Goodies and Daddies

Goodies and Daddies is a funny and practical guide to fatherhood. Blooded in the battle of the baby manuals, Michael Rosen – father of five – tackles everything from the ticklish ('Babies' Blotches') to the tempestuous ('Bathtime'), not forgetting that simply 'Being Around' is one of the most important aspects of being a hands-on father.

This book will make you laugh, even if it won't turn you into the world's best dad or sit up with your screaming one-year-old five nights on the trot. And the alphabetical order makes it a perfect dip-read for those quiet moments . . .

For fathers of all varieties it makes an ideal gift. Whether New Man or shameless diehard, a dip into the wit and wisdom of *Goodies and Daddies* will show you the clearings in the jungle of fatherhood.

Michael Rosen is a writer, poet, performer and broadcaster. His hugely popular books of children's poetry are worldwide best-sellers.

D1385149

Other books by the author

For very young children

You Can't Catch Me
Don't Put Mustard in the Custard
Under the Bed
Hard Boiled Legs
Smelly Jelly Smelly Fish
Spollyollydiddlytiddlyitis

For adults

Did I Hear You Write?
The Chatto Book of Dissent
(with David Widgery)

Goodies and Daddies

An A–Z Guide to Fatherhood

Michael Rosen

Illustrations by Caroline Holden

John Murray

© Michael Rosen 1991

First published in 1991
by John Murray (Publishers) Ltd
50 Albemarle Street, London W1X 4BD

Reprinted in paperback 1992, 1993, 1995

The right of Michael Rosen to be
identified as the author of this work has
been asserted by him in accordance with
the Copyright, Designs and Patents Act,
1988.

All rights reserved
Unauthorized duplication
contravenes applicable laws

British Library Cataloguing-in-Publication-Data

Rosen, Michael
  Goodies and Daddies: An A-Z guide to fatherhood.
  I. Title
  649

  ISBN 0–7195–5161–7

Typeset in 11 on 13pt Palatino by Wearset, Boldon, Tyne & Wear
Printed in Great Britain by
Athenæum Press Ltd, Gateshead, Tyne & Wear

For Geraldine, Joe, Naomi, Eddie, Laura and Isaac

Contents

Dad winking by Isaac (aged 3).

Introduction

A quick trip along the shelves marked Health in a bookshop, will bring you up sharp against a large number of books to do with having babies, looking after babies, wishing you had babies; coping with madly clever babies, cleverly mad babies, bad babies, sad babies; food for babies that will make them clever, food for babies that will make them mad; outings for babies, illnesses for babies . . . and nearly all of them are written for women.

There is a rumour going round that men sometimes get involved in some of this, and even that it's become a habit in some homes. On the other hand, there are also rumours that nothing's really changed, it's just that a lot of people, especially women, wish that it had.

With this state of affairs in mind, I've written a book that is about looking after babies and young children. It's for men and it's written by a man, but of course it can easily be bought by a woman with all kinds of hopes in her mind.

I am not a doctor, therapist, counsellor, or guru. I am a writer of children's books and a father and step-father to five children who as I write are aged 14, 12, 10, 7 and 3. I've been married twice, the first time producing two boys (14 and 10), the second time introducing me first to two step-daughters (12 and 7) and then producing a boy of our own (3). This has been described to me as a 'blended family', but maybe that's because when we met we each had a blender . . . It also gives rise to the complaint by one of us: 'Your children are fighting my children and our child started it.'

What follows is a collection of thoughts, memories and tips

based on the past fourteen years. It's in alphabetical order, which seems a suitably random form to express the haphazard way in which delights and problems confront a parent. If I had tried to write the book as a continuous narrative, I don't think anyone would have stayed the course; but assembled like this, I hope a reader will dip-read it on the loo, waiting for a bus, cooking, while the ads come on in the middle of a film, or with the baby on one arm.

The fathering I'm talking about here is not the whole course from soup to nuts. I'm restricting myself to 0 to 5, though as you'll see, children as old as my fourteen-year-old make occasional appearances.

I don't promise any easy solutions; it's not a Dad Construction Kit, where all you have to do is follow the instructions and stick together the relevant parts with a non-toxic glue. In a world where men had had as long a tradition of looking after babies and young children as women, such a book would hardly be necessary – we would just talk to each other. In a world where men who do get involved in such things are often separated by miles and by deep-seated inhibitions, I hope this book will give you confidence, strength and the occasional laugh.

I've tried not to sound bossy – it's a common disease in the battle-worn parent looking at the newcomer. Just grit your teeth when I come on a bit strong and tell yourself that I mean well. I would love to have been able to thank some men for having shown me ways in which to look after young children, but the person who taught me the most was an elderly working-class Irish woman, my first wife's mother, whom my boys knew as Nanna.

Babies' Blotches

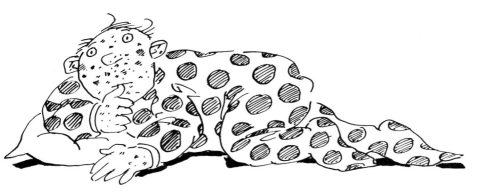

Babies in ads are smooth and shiny and glowing – beware! Real babies are often blotchy and flaky. Rashes and blobs appear all over them for no apparent reason. You worry that if you go out with your baby covered in spots people will think it's scurvy or – even worse – it's caused by dirty sheets and male incompetence. ('Tut, tut, if that child had its mother looking after it then it wouldn't have scurvy.') At times I've found myself behaving like some mad explorer, spending whole evenings poring over the islands and seas on a baby's skin.

Other people's babies' blotches always look worse than your baby's. In fact, given that they look so beastly, you can never quite figure out how other parents can possibly love their children. However, just in case you get concerned about your one's spots, here's my journal of discovery.

Sometimes the blotches were pin-points, sometimes splodges, sometimes little white bumps on the face, and sometimes scabby things on his head. (All this as well as NAPPY RASH!) I soon discovered that none of these was leprosy, ringworm, measles or even German measles.

The pin-points were heat rashes. In hot weather, two or three of my children have come up in heat rashes. They differ from the two measles in that they don't spread evenly round behind the ears and across the chest, but erupt in little groups of pin-points anywhere they're hot, like in the crease of the neck, where the clothes are tight, or randomly across the chest. Sponging with cool water is the quickest way to deal with them, but it's more important that they're drinking loads.

Splodges have always been a mystery. At various times I've thought it was soap, the dressing in a new vest, something they'd eaten, a reaction to traffic pollution, a detergent, and so on. They seemed to come and go over a day or so. If it is an allergy, you can try to eliminate the possibilities by going through all the different foods and possible irritants. One Sunday afternoon my second child pigged out on satsumas and the next day he came out in red blotches, round his ribs. That was how we discovered he was allergic to citrus.

White bumps on the face, I was told by various old ladies, were 'milk buds'. They don't matter at all. Scabby things on the head *do* matter, because if they get too widespread, the skin can crack and make the scalp bleed. It's called 'cradle cap'. It's a bit of a drag but the best way to deal with it is very gently to massage an oil into the scalp, leave it for as long as is convenient, shampoo it out, and then brush very gently. You may have to do this once a week for a bit, if it's got bad.

Ringworm does still exist; my citrus-allergic child seems prone to getting it (he seems to be up for any fungus going, actually) and babies can catch it from older children who've picked it up in school. Look out for a single ring-shaped weal, with a different colour in the middle, or a patch of white flakey stuff on the head with hair loss in the middle of it (unlike cradle cap, which tends to go brown). This is one for the doctor. I've found that doctors are really keen on spotty children, who give them loads of things to look up, and lots of interesting questions to ask.

All this is very different from eczema, and should not be taken as minimizing the worry and trouble children and parents go through with this. None of my children has had it, so I won't pretend to be an expert.

Babysitters

I've found that the worst thing about babysitters is that you book them several days before you want to go out, but by the time the day comes round for them to babysit, you're too shattered to want to go out. Too late: they're booked, they come, you go out and sit down in the restaurant, and fall asleep.

I always used to think that records-and-clothes-hungry teenagers would be the most ideal babysitters. Surely they would queue up to come over to watch your telly, eat your cake, and go home with a few quid in their pockets? Not so. All the ones we've had are OK for a few times but then suddenly reveal in some subtle way ('Going out tonight, aren't I?') that they've got their own lives to lead. The other problem with teenagers is that they can lose their grip. One nice lad spent all evening trying to get our three-year-old to bed. She just sat on the sofa staring at him. In the end the poor lad rang his mum, who told him to keep calm. When we got in at well past eleven our little treasure was still there, bright and smiley. The boys, when they were little, all went in for outrageous flirting with the teenage girls and young women – lots of blushing and running around giggling and dropping of pyjama bottoms. Small wonder some of those sitters never came back.

I reckon the worst arrangement is the old ticket system where you have a babysitters' circle. It leads to partners arguing over who's going to do it, or somebody builds up a backlog of tickets and you get to feeling like you want to go round and punch them on the nose. In fact, arguing over whose turn it is, and whether a Sunday morning counts as much as a Saturday night, is one of the quickest ways to lose friends.

By far the best set-up we've had so far is an agency. Everyone needs everyone else in the arrangement; the boss of the agency needs people who are reliable or they get the hoof, the babysitters have made a conscious decision that they need the money and they aren't doing anyone a favour, and you get someone who turns up on time and does the business. If not, you complain. The young woman who comes at the moment is a vegan, and as a result our children have taken to saying things like 'Hamburgers are dead cows, aren't they, Dad?'

Bathtime

I have a photo of myself surrounded by a group of schoolgirls in a child development class watching me bath my first child. The girls are looking on in amazement and horror. This is partly because they're thinking I'm a clumsy old twit who's likely to drop the baby any minute. The other reason is that they are all black, and this is the first time they have ever seen a naked white baby. They were horrified that you could see his veins.

Bathing babies is a tricky business. They are very small and very slippery. This may well sound like an evil heresy to your women mentors, but you don't actually have to *bath* babies. You can lay them on your lap, on a towel, and sponge them down with warm water and hug them dry. Then you don't have to go in for that game of feeling the water with your elbow, supporting the baby with one hand while you try and wash it with the other, all the time putting your fingers in your ears so you can't hear the screaming.

As for bathing: if, like me, you've got big hands, it's a great help. It's really nice getting the baby to play with the water. Do everything slowly and gently; a non-skid mat in the bath is a great help. If you're going to talc them afterwards, don't puff the powder all over them – it only gets into their lungs. Try and avoid extremes of temperature getting in and out of the bath and bathroom (another reason for avoiding it altogether).

When they get older, then it's time to stock up on bath toys. I've found this is a great time to re-live all the nutty things I used to do in the bath when I was a kid. I've taught my kids about drip races, tidal waves, and how to make bubble submarines with the flannel . . . bliss! There's a huge range of toys in the shops involving little blokes diving in, wheels going round, hippopotamuses zooming round in circles, and so on. All jolly good fun, and great solutions to the birthday and Christmas presents problem. Yoghurt pots, plastic bottles, ice cream boxes, bits of wood, lufas, pumice, and the like all have great potential too, and they are all a great distraction from the hell that is called HAIRWASHING.

Bedtime

'But I'm not tired ... can I stay up and watch the football? ...
Tell that story about the time you got lost, Dad ... one more
game of draughts ...'

It's one of the great family battlefields. Just as everyone is
getting tired and ratty there's a whole heap of fiddly, even
more tiring things to be done. Kids see the jugular and go for it.
They are geniuses at devising new ways of delaying bedtime. If
you could do an A-level in bedtime-delaying routines, all kids

under five would pass. I reckon this is a time when democracy has to go out the window. Let's say, that, like us, you do a two-biscuits-before-bed routine. Any child over the age of eighteen months knows how choosing biscuits can take up to ten minutes. You'll end up swearing that you'll never buy a Figgy Roll again. As with any other stage on the journey to bed, you can try one of two things: 1.   offer no choices and, in this case, slam two biscuits down and close the tin quick; 2.   say, 'Time for biscuits. You have five seconds to choose or there *are* no biscuits! One, two, threeeeeee, foooooooour, fiiiiiiiiiiiiiiiiive', and again, slam the tin shut quick. It's brutal, but it works.

I've applied this system to bath bubbles, choosing a story book, finding teddies, kissing brothers and sisters goodnight. If I don't, I end up a shattered wreck with no evening left.

Bedtime routines are generally reckoned to be a good idea. It's obviously nice for children to know that there is a set of comforting stages to go through on the way to that strange and lonely place called bed. Going to bed means going to sleep, which means saying goodbye, and no one likes saying goodbye to loved ones, no matter how old you are.

If you're the kind of father who gets home at around bedtime then you may well think that the last thing you can face is playing flannel-submarines and reading *Mrs Tiggywinkle*. The problem is that your partner thinks exactly the same thing. She may have spent the last few hours coping with tantrums, baked beans on the floor, and three pooey nappies. Or she may have spent the last few hours coping with tantrums and the rest at work. So even though your feet feel like someone very large has spent all day jumping on them, now is your chance to get into childcare. If women ever *have* dreamed of men arriving at the door and whisking them away on dashing white chargers, then you turning up and offering to squeeze a kid or two into pyjamas is a very close second best.

I mentioned reading a book as part of the bedtime routine. Perhaps I don't need to wax lyrical about this, but I will anyway. You snuggle up on the sofa with a newly bathed infant, all hot and sweet-smelling, you choose a book between you, and right there you witness the discovery that words and pictures can tickle you pink, terrify you, sadden you, intrigue

you, and so on. And remember, learning to read is not simply the business of deciphering a code ('that letter is ''b'' and that makes a ''b''-sound'). We have to show children that reading is something interesting and pleasurable. With very young children, when we read to them at bedtime we are, among other things, introducing them to the conventions of the book: how books work from left to right, how stories unfold, how pictures and words tell two complementary stories, how the title is on the cover, the fact that it's people called writers and illustrators who make books, and how they have their own styles and so on. All these things we take for granted, but as you're cuddling up on the sofa, it's all going on in the child's mind.

As the late arriver in the house of an evening, this might be the only time you get to see your children before bedtime. So you've got to squeeze all that love and care into one reading of *Where the Wild Things Are* or *Peter Rabbit*.

Go for it! Remember how they didn't want you in the school play? Remember how your dad told you to shut up singing in the bath? Not any more. Now you have a captive audience. You can dish up every mad voice, crazy face and loony noise that you've ever invented. Children's books are full of grotesques, talking animals, fools, villains, goody-goodies, wind, police sirens, raspberries . . . it's fantastic. Give it all you've got and even if it's pathetic, they'll still love you for it.

Sometimes the words in the stories are too hard. No problem, change them or explain them. Keep the flow of the story going, but don't shout down the questions that your child asks you. It's all vital pre-reading stuff. Be prepared to talk about pictures, pointing out interesting bits. Watch out for scarey things; there's nothing wrong with a bit of a scare, but the child needs a safety net to fall into. You may have to do a lot of reassuring, but that's no bad thing. Stories are often about being reassured that if you oppose badness and danger you can survive. Children want to know whether they can survive as well. And a good time to find out, is just before you go to sleep.

See also READING BOOKS

Bedwetting

Beware of bedwetting bores! You only have to breathe a word that one of your children has wet the bed and they come at you like a hurricane. You soon discover that what they're really on about is *shame*. They remember wetting the bed when they were children, they remember their mums or dads getting all screwed up about it and moaning about soggy, smelly sheets. They had children and whaddayaknow? – they got all screwed up about it, too. Then you come along and happen to mention that one of your kids wet the bed last night and – whoosh! they hit you with a great heap of shame dressed up as advice.

If you are armed with a plastic undersheet, a washing machine and big child-sized nappies, bedwetting doesn't have to be a problem as far as mess is concerned. Remember, some people call it a bedwetting problem when it is really that they're not prepared to let their child wear night-nappies for as long as they want or need. The point is that, if a child is over about three and still not dry at nights, the child itself can increasingly take on more and more responsibility about wearing the nappies: buying them, putting them on, taking them off, throwing them away and so on. In fact, the very business of taking charge of the process might help, in the long run, to get the child dry.

We let one of our children wear a night nappy till she was over six because that's what she needed to do. She then very much wanted to get out of wearing them and said several times, unsuccessfully, 'No nappy tonight.' Eventually, I think it was the fact that she discovered she could get up in the night, go to the toilet on her own and put herself back to bed that helped to get her dry.

It doesn't need me to say that some children who have been dry at night but then begin to bed-wet do it as part of some kind of crisis. In situations like this, suggesting the wearing of nappies at night would be, in effect, punishing them, and that's the last thing you want to do. However, if the choice is between being a cold, wet, smelly person and wearing nappies, then it might help. The most important thing, though, is to try to find out where the anxieties are, and relieve them. The hardest thing to cope with is thinking or knowing that you might be the cause of the anxieties: have I been making too heavy demands on her? Expecting her to succeed too much? Are the rows between me and my partner causing it? Is something going on at school that I don't know about? Or it may just be that the child is saying she wants you to spend more time with her. Hmmmmm.

As a footnote: the worst aspect of women being restricted to a domestic role is that this seems to have induced areas of pride where they are least appropriate. So, it becomes a matter of pride that a child doesn't wet the bed. A bedwetting child is a slur on motherhood. Ideally, the great thing about being a bloke and getting involved with things like this means that you don't have to carry this burden. Your kid wets the bed? So he wets the bed. If you're into male competitiveness, then stick to golf and Volvos. Don't turn Monday morning at work into driest bed competitions; it'll be the child that suffers.

Being Around

If I had to say what I thought was one of the most important things about being a dad, it is 'being around'. The worst thing about being a father is that too often, for real or imagined reasons, you have to be out working. Being around means that you are somewhere in the house being available for rows, cuddles, crises, laughs, food, mess and the rest. I've found it very easy to categorize all kinds of little tasks, like fetching children from school, doing shopping with them, feeding them when they're young, as 'not needing my presence'. If they don't need my presence, then I can be elsewhere in the house. If I can be elsewhere in the house, I don't really have to be home at all, and because I don't have my partner's undivided attention I might as well be out having a good time or working somewhere else.

What follows from this is that sometimes the only way you can programme yourself to be around is to take on trivial little tasks like wiping the table or tidying the mantelpiece (or try the trivial big tasks like doing the washing and cleaning the loo), and I've found that it's during these times that you actually make a relationship with your children. It's then that they ask you the really important things, like 'Why do you pee standing up?' or 'Do buffaloes eat spaghetti?' and other vital questions.

Even if you don't do the trivial tasks but you're just *there*, reading the paper, your presence is a great big affirmation that you like the company you're keeping, just as your absence creates the tiny anxiety that home isn't where you want to be and the children aren't who you want to be with. If you are just around, then children will claim you, even if you don't get into

the business of claiming them. I have two step-daughters whom I didn't make enormous efforts to befriend and love, partly because I was so worried that the separation from my first wife was affecting my own 'natural' children. The step-daughters have always had other ideas, and once it became clear I wasn't the enemy, they started making claims on me as a dad. They can only do that if I'm there to be climbed on and argued with.

See also CRAZES, GETTING AWAY

Birth

I'm not going to pretend to be an expert on birth: I'll just tell the stories of the three births I've been at. The first and second were hospital births and the third was at home.

For the first, I went along to ante-natal classes at the hospital where a kind but rather inhibited fifty-year-old woman told us about how the baby grows and gave my partner some exercises to do which I had to do with her. This mostly seemed to involve crawling round the floor on all fours arching our backs, and squeezing each other's arms till it hurt.

Plenty of men find these classes excruciating. In the normal run of pregnancy you may feel irrelevant and pretty useless and then, just to rub it in, you have to turn up in public as the labelled sidekick. 'Ah-hah,' say some women, 'now you know what it feels like to have to go to your work-place parties, and your friends' dos . . .'. How much value you get out of these classes is closely related to what kind of birth you and your partner have in mind. If you're planning on having a hi-tech, conveyor belt, production-line job, then the birth will mostly turn on the machines and minds of the medics. Your role will be smiling, forehead-mopping and phoning the relatives. The more active a birth the pair of you envisage, the greater your role will be. Instead of just nodding keenly, you may find yourself learning bum-massage, belly-oiling, controlled breathing and something called 'supported squats'. Some of this is part of making the pregnancy-time more enjoyable (if that's the right word), and some of it is to do with rehearsing for the birth itself. In this first birth I was involved with, we either didn't know, or didn't try to know, how we could have done more

about making the pregnancy something *we* were going through
– rather than something that doctors were administering for us.

The last two weeks of this first pregnancy were hell for her
and she lay about in the corner of the room moaning and
waiting. I had no idea what to do about this, and just kept
bobbing up and down hopelessly making encouraging noises
and feeling guilty that it was somehow my fault. It was at times
like these that knowing about massage and the like would have
made us feel less helpless. (Nowadays, there's a clutch of books
on the market including sections on massage in pregnancy.)

We knew when the baby was due because we timed the
length of time between contractions (when they're regular, and
frequent), and an ambulance came to pick us up. Two weeks
before I had done the suitcase bit: packing all the things she
would need in hospital. She couldn't face that because it
seemed too committed. I had a role at last: suitcase-packer-in-
chief.

When it came to the actual thing, she was stretched out on
her back, in what seemed like an operating theatre, on the
hottest day for half a century. The baby seemed to get stuck,
the doctor kept shouting 'push in the bottom! push in the
bottom!', while my partner had me in a kind of neck lock which
meant that for most of the labour my nose was in her armpit.
The number of people in the room went up and up until there
seemed to be a whole crowd of people peering and waiting. A
woman in a short white coat appeared and said: 'Go on, you
can do it', there was some shouting about the cord, and the
baby came out. There were more mutterings about the cord,
which I discovered some hours later meant that it had been
round the baby's neck, but the doctor didn't have time to
explain because he had rushed out of the room to see if the
eggs in the pigeon's nest on the balcony had hatched. They
had, and he was very very excited.

All in all, it had been confusing and worrying. Why did more
and more people start coming into the room? They weren't
students, one of them was an oldish bloke in a blazer. Why did
the baby seem to get stuck? All that shouting about push
harder seemed to be saying that somehow my partner wasn't
doing enough. I think, to be absolutely honest, I thought that

too. Note here: it is terribly easy, as a man, to side with all the men in the room. 'We chaps know how this is done . . . just get on with it, woman, don't be so damned feeble . . .' etc., etc. In actual fact, there was a mini-crisis here: the cord being round the baby's neck is a problem, which in this case was solved by the doctor putting his hand inside and doing a nifty bit of girl-guide knot-work to free the baby. Why wasn't this explained to us? If not during, then after? Perhaps I wasn't bold enough at the time to ask questions. If you don't want the event to be remembered as mysterious and irritating – ask questions. Part of being pleased about having a baby is knowing how it survived the first trial of life.

The next birth started when 'the waters broke', which I discovered sounded like someone tipping out a bucket. The hospital ordered us in straight away and soon we were on the conveyor belt where doctors, midwives and nurses tell you of one inevitable consequence after another – none of which, are you allowed to think at the time, presents any alternative course of action. Because the waters had broken they said the birth was due, even though labour pains hadn't begun. When the labour didn't start, they said to delay any longer would cause infection so they would have to induce. To induce, they put her on a drip. When this didn't work, because they used the wrong dose of drip, they had to hurry the whole thing up with a double dose of drip. Needless to say, the birth itself I can scarcely remember.

In situations like this you are in the worst of all worlds. Without any other source of advice you find yourself nodding and agreeing to everything, even though each one of these steps is debatable and other courses of action are possible. In our case we also experienced the medical cock-up of the induction dose being too low, and so there were several hours of pointless (dangerous?) stress. No one felt it necessary to apologize to us about this; there were just a few hurried mutterings between doctors and nurses, and rapid readjustments. None of this matters if you and your partner are people who want this period in your lives to be done *to* you rather than *by* you. I've felt like this at times. But if you want this time to be something you have some control over, then it is precisely at the moment when doctors are talking injections and inductions that *you* have a role. The key issue is: are the medics taking decisions for their convenience, or for your partner's and yours? If you think it is mostly for their convenience, then basically it's down to you to intervene because your partner will probably be too far gone, too woozy and too preoccupied with herself to be able to take on the medics, too. This is . . . Responsibility. Something I know I didn't take on during this second birth.

The third birth I was at was with my second wife, who wanted to have this her third baby at home – just as she had had her second. The plan was to have an independent midwife and doctor to attend the birth. I think we assumed that the birth would happen in the bedroom. As the contractions started coming naturally we did the un-hippy thing of ushering the children off next door, rang the midwife, and waited. My wife then started walking around the bedroom and I massaged the base of her back. I remember feeling very calm, even madly so, when it slowly crossed my mind that we might be the only ones around when the baby came into the world. I found myself imagining catching babies, footballs, and a Christmas pudding I had once dropped. Every now and then we took a quick peek out of the window to see if there was any sign of the midwife, and then the groaning and swearing started up. (Not from me. I've since been told this is definitely normal!) Just then, the midwife did arrive and my partner rushed off to the loo. The midwife signed me to keep an eye on what was going on, and next thing my partner shouted 'I can feel it at the front!' She knelt forward while I sat on the edge of the bath, the midwife came in and spread a few old terry towels on the floor, and out came the baby.

This was the pregnancy and birth that was the most planned of the three. My wife knew what she wanted to do in the birth, to have it at home and have it in whatever position she would feel most comfortable at the time: squatting, crawling, half-squatting or however. She was also clear about what she wanted from me, in terms of helping her get into those positions, and massaging her. (She didn't ask for ice-packs on her sacrum, but some women find that a great relief.) Having an independent midwife was a great luxury, and she and her doctor colleague were wonderful in supporting the idea that the birth was something *we* did that they supervised, rather than administered. They were also great with our children, spending a lot of time checking dollies' blood pressure and heart beats.

This pregnancy was the first where I felt I got really involved with helping with food. I'm told many women find preparing food either nauseating or an emotional burden (having to think about other people when they would quite like to think about themselves). On top of that, women are bombarded with advice: no booze, no fags, plenty of calcium foods – milk and chick peas (houmous, falafel) – heaps of fresh food, iron-rich foods like beetroot and grapes, plenty of fish. If any or all of this means a break from what she was eating before, then it's a great help if you share it too.

All three of my children are boys (what's the matter with me? have I only got XY chromosomes?), and one feeling I had in relation to all three is how amazed I was that such a large and complete human being comes out. One moment there's no one, and the next something alive and whole appears in the world. At the very moment of birth I don't think I felt that the baby was much to do with me. In each case it took a few days of cuddling, looking, and thinking before I felt it was.

A frequent worry is that the birth itself will be something very violent and bloody. Some people are very worried about pain, sometimes more worried about other people's pain than their own. There's no point in pretending that birth is like going down a slide. Of course there's blood – and sometimes shit and piss, too, but basically that's the human condition. It always strikes me that accepting and even enjoying this side of life is much less undignified than trying to sanitize it and ignore it. Of course, it may be that you have just the same feelings, but when it actually comes to it, you can't help yourself passing out, like many others before you. Remember, there is sometimes quite a good physical reason for this – such as that you haven't eaten or drunk anything for about seven hours, and you've been sitting in some funny position for a lot of the time.

A well-kept secret of mine is that I spent a short time in my life wondering if I would be a doctor. This meant that I did a year of a degree in physiology. I let you in on this exciting fact to explain why I find it very easy to overlook other people's ignorance about how bodies, and in this case ovaries, wombs and vaginas, actually work. I'm not going to sit here and say that every expectant father should read a text book on birth, but you could make a bit of an effort to find out how it all works, if only for the reason that your partner will take this to mean you're interested in what she's going through. It also means you can offer views on what doctors and midwives are saying, when your partner comes back from check-ups. If you think you know it all anyway, here's a quick test: what are the following – the cervix, the second stage, amniotic fluid, and the placenta?

Looking back on all three events, I find I am irritated by how calm I was at the time of the birth itself. Perhaps the calmness was a defence. The actual arrival of a new and very small human being sometimes seems too quick for something that affects your life for so long afterwards. To be honest, I didn't feel very useful at any of the births; I never felt I was doing something special or particular that no other person could have done. None of this is intended to deny that other men have felt exhilarated, excited, and needed or, alternatively, frightened, angry, or shocked. Sitting in the calm of remembering, I feel proud I was there, and warm that I know what my children looked like when they were one second old. As far as relationships with partners are concerned, I don't feel anything mystical or extra-close happened but, of course, if I hadn't been there it would probably have been very nastily disruptive and negative. In one sense I feel more kind of old-soldierish about it: I was there, doing my stuff, and I'm here now to talk about it. I suppose it's a feeling that says: I was reliable, wasn't I? Which feels nice, but a bit boring!

Birthdays

Birthdays are brilliant. Go mad, have cakes, ice cream, chocolate fingers, flash photos, in-laws, balloons, crisps – but don't, *don't* invite hundreds of children. Either you or your partner will ignore this advice, dismissing me as a miserable Scrooge, and you will tell me that making four hundred cucumber sandwiches and playing Pass-the-Parcel was fun. You will have turned a blind eye to the fight over the party-poppers between your little one-year-old and the huge brutal two-year-old next door. You will have ignored the meringue ground into the 100 per cent wool job on the sitting-room floor.

We've institutionalized birthdays to a Sunday tea-time with a visit to the local posh 24-hour deli where they sell things like damson ice cream, tortilla chips and Black Forest cheesecake. In-laws and neighbours can come if they want to, and the odd friend here and there. Anything more than that and we'd go mad.

A father's role at parties is to eat lots of ice cream.

See CHILDREN'S PARTIES

Car Journeys

'Now listen, I can't drive properly with that noise. If there's one more squeak out of them I'm going to stop the car. I can't stand the noise. Why don't they just look out of the window? Give her a drink if she wants one. Who's been sick? Where? Of course I can't stop here. Open the windows. Yes, I do want the radio on, I'm waiting for the cricket score. Well, we would be making good time if we didn't have to keep stopping. Didn't you bring a book she could look at? Yes, I know it makes her sick, but everything makes her sick. I'm not shouting. Isn't she old enough to listen to a tape or something? ... She'll be wearing silk pyjamas when she comes, singin' ay ay yippee, singin' ay ay yippee yippee ay ... there's another blue car, there's another one – see, that makes three blue cars. Now why's she crying? Of course we're nearly there, if she asks are we nearly there once more, I'm going to stop the car, jump out and go for a run in that field ... she hasn't sat on that marker pen, has she? I know it's the waterproof one ... any of those cakes for me? Oh, I missed out on those, did I? Don't let her go to sleep now, she'll never go to bed when we get there ... uh-huh there's a hold-up.'

See also CAR SEATS

Children in your Bed

One of my children managed every night, one way or another, to end up in our bed. This would have been bad enough, but he also managed to end up sleeping with his feet in my ear. And they twitched. Like a lot of other parents, I've had children who've been desperate to be in the bed and never want to leave and others who never really discovered the pleasure and aren't that bothered about it. There are no rules, here.

Starting with the baby . . . do you have the baby in the bed? Factors affecting this decision are: do you have a huge bed? Do you believe that babies need body contact for at least the whole of the first year (the so-called continuum effect)? Do you mind having it off while a baby's in the bed? Babies certainly like being in your bed, but then some people find it difficult ever to get them out. If you object but your partner thinks it's a good idea, ask yourself whether you are against it only because you're jealous of someone else being in her arms (see JEALOUSY). If your partner objects but you think it would be a good idea because you've read a book about it, then tough! It's her milk the baby's after, and if your partner would rather not have the baby nuzzling for it all night, there's not much you can do about it.

As the children get older, many (perhaps most?) parents seem to let them into bed in the mornings, if only at the weekend. There's plenty of stroppy fourteen-year-olds that secretly yearn for this and would jump at the chance if they knew you would say yes and not laugh at them for it. My ten-year-old boy loves it.

Children's Parties

Don't.

See BIRTHDAYS

Cot Moving

A traditional pattern of sleeping arrangements goes like this: newborn baby in carry cot beside your bed so that she can be lifted quickly to be fed in the night. After a while she moves on to having her own cot, on the other side of the room. After a further while, the cot gets moved into a separate room. And last step, after yet further time, is to move the child into a bed.

There are no rules about this sequence – whether you follow it, or not – nor on how long each stage is. Some people have the baby in with them, some people put the newborn baby straight away in a cot on its own in another room. Some people believe that a baby needs almost permanent body contact with another human for around a whole year. Others say that if you teach a baby right from the start to sleep in its own cot in another room, you'll have tranquil nights and a long and happy life. It's an emotional matter, and men tend towards the put-her-in-the-other-room approach while women tend to be more tolerant of the near-at-hand method.

You may hear all kinds of advice on this matter from other parents, your own parents, from books – but in the end, the solution you come up with has to suit your way of life and your emotional outlook. If you try to do something you don't agree with but someone has told you works wonders, then it won't work for you. This is A Thought.

Crazes

My mother had a devastating line: when one of us mentioned a man we knew, she would say, 'Ten!', or 'Eight!' She wasn't giving them marks out of ten – she was describing their mental age. It was only a variation on the old gag about men being little boys. It would crop up mostly because she had heard about some man or another pursuing a craze.

The crunch for us here is when it's Craze versus Childcare. When deep down you know it's your turn to take them to Woolworths, is it really necessary to lock yourself in the darkroom, inspect the fishing flies, or mend the model railway lines? I've noticed how apparently useful tasks like decorating, car maintenance, gardening and the like can be used as a smokescreen for avoiding childcare. DIY can be prolonged for the whole of the time the children are growing up: there's the Sunday morning skip inspection where you really *do* have to poke around in the area's skips to see if tiles, sinks, and wood (always wood) can be salvaged. There's the Saturday afternoon trek to the DIY shops, where long chats about Philips screwdrivers must, but must, be had with those blokes in overalls. And there's the disasters: the wallpaper that doesn't stick, the paint that doesn't match, the cupboards that collapse. It all takes hours and hours and hours, it's all much too dangerous for the kids to help with, and it's all supposedly desperately necessary – 'I'm keeping the home together here, love.'

Dad's Back

If you're in a traditional set-up, out working while your wife looks after the children, then 'Dad's back!' is a moment full of emotion: 'Yippee, he's back, now we'll have some fun', 'Oh what a pity he isn't here more', 'It's all very well for him to come home and have fun with the kids, I have to do all the hard slog all day and he gets the fun stuff', 'I'm completely shattered from all that boring stuff at work and now I'm supposed to be all cheery and hearty the moment I walk through the door', 'I can't stand the noise', 'Look out when your father gets in, he's often tired, hungry and grumpy', 'Have you brought us any presents?'

Then there's stories to be caught up on, and the problem with the minder, the washing machine, the next-door-neighbour's cat, the little one's earache and the lack of buses into town. It's an awful lot of stuff, all jammed into one moment. Ideal for sparking off a row because someone, including you, thinks that someone else is not listening, not caring enough, not being nice enough. Someone might well have a shout and stomp off.

For one man I knew, who lived next door to my parents, coming home was the opposite of all this. It was the only moment in the day he felt truly happy. The moment he was through the door, he was on the floor with the toys. He thought it was the only thing he did in life that was worth anything. I'll never forget the expression on his face when I once said something about the kids growing up quickly. He looked devastated.

Dad's Bum and Dad's Trousers

Women know only too well that it's hard to think about why you should look OK when you're concentrating on someone else. You see, you might take all this fathering business to heart and take it on really seriously, only to discover that you've been attacked by the twin diseases of 'Dad's Bum' and 'Dad's Trousers'. The first indications of the illness might come from your kids. You're bending down or squatting to pick up toys scattered all over the floor when one of your kids says, 'Dad, your bum's all squodgy!' Perhaps they glimpsed it through split pockets, or bulging out of trouser tops as in Plumbers' Cheeks. Everyone gets a good laugh out of it. Don't get ratty with them – they know not what pain they're causing. And it's no use pretending it's because the jumper's too short. Long jumpers hide Dad's Bum but don't remove it, and there's a possibility that its appearance at the bedside has a distinctly dampening effect on the partner's hormones. Beware!

The tatty trousers that should have been changed yesterday go with Dad's Bum – the symptoms here are the saggy crotch and the split pocket. I must admit, I have been suffering from both Dad's Bum and Dad's Trousers for something like fifteen years: I gather that there are remedies to be found in jogging, swimming, and trips to flash jeans shops.

Drawing on Walls

I have yet to meet a child who hasn't at one time or another scribbled on the wall. I remember once when my dad came up to kiss me goodnight, just as I was getting going on the wall next to my bed. In a panic I sat up and tried to cover it. My dad stopped for a little chat while I sat there twisted up against the wall, trying to look natural. After a bit my dad noticed that I hadn't moved from this strange position, and interrupted himself in the middle of the chat to say, 'Hey, what are you hiding there?' 'Nothing, it's OK.' 'No, come on, I can see you're hiding something,' he says, still cheery. I couldn't hide it any longer, and leaned forward. He went bananas. I was about ten at the time.

With little tiny ones, there isn't much point in getting mad at them. You've spent all that time sticking pens and crayons and pencils in front of them. You've applauded every little scribble, you've pinned up the masterpieces ON THE WALL. They put two and two together: great scribbles go on the wall. Why don't I do a short-cut, and get scribbling straight onto it?

One solution to the problem I saw was pinning up lining paper horizontally along the child's bedroom wall. It was a great idea, but it was just loose enough to allow for felt tips to go straight through onto the wall behind.

Lots of 'the only place we draw is on this kind of paper' is in order here, and lightning reactions. More child-centred people assume the worst and suspend all ideas of home beaut. (as the Australians call it) until children leave home.

Dressing

Trying to dress a baby for the first time can be a frightening experience. You think you've pulled an arm off, a finger's got left behind in a babygrow, or a suffocation has taken place under a vest. Dressing a baby is like dressing a screaming rubber doll. First rule: don't do it with anyone watching. It'll take you twice as long and you'll probably end up putting a vest on its legs. Second rule: watch the experts at work and see how they do it. Notice how they hold the arms to get them into the sleeves, which way round the baby is facing at each point in the operation, which way onto the head the vest goes, and listen to the reassuring noises that are being made as the whole thing gets under way.

For those who have no experts to watch, here are some tips:

- When babies are very young you have to dress them as they are lying down, but the moment they begin to sit up you can sit them on your lap, back firmly against your belly, and dress them like that.

- Putting on clothes that go over the heads (vests, jumpers, etc.) must be done by approaching the baby's head from behind. Make the neck-hole of the vest fit over the bump that sticks out of the back of the head, and pull from there. Taking the same garment off, you lift from the front, up over the chin, face, forehead, and off. I'm not one for rules and laws, but this certainly is one. Doing it the wrong way can be painful.

- Putting hands into sleeves is done by you holding the hand

and going down the sleeve with the baby's hand as far as you can go; same with feet and legs.

- In cold weather, woollen vests next to the skin are worth two jumpers on top. Hats, gloves and booties are vital for at least nine months of the year in England.

- Children find dressing very boring except when they can annoy you. So they try running away, hiding their hands and making their feet stick out at a funny angle. Sometimes they grow extra arms. Hit back with tricks and jokes. Try the 'Bye-bye hand' routine: as the hand disappears into the sleeve, pull it out quickly, half a millimetre from your nose, feigning huge surprise. Try the same with the feet. Snags with this: you may have to repeat it every day for four years. Other routines: putting knickers on child's head – or yours (never fails, this one) – and producing lost socks from behind child's ear.

I'm hopelessly sexist about buying clothes, leaving it all to my partner, but have at times made efforts. I have to admit that, when I was more conscientious about it, it was very pleasing buying clothes that looked nice on a young child or, even better, that they said they liked. I was more confident in areas like pyjamas and tee shirts, but I have occasionally graduated to track suit bottoms and shoes. Skirts and dresses – can't manage at all. One thing that intimidated me was that every time I bought something for my second son, it was OK in the shop but by the time he got home, he had grown out of it. The moral of this story is never to take any notice of the signs or labels that say '2–3 years' and the like. Buy big – in a week the garment's shrunk and the baby's grown. If it's really madly too big, it'll fit next year.

Women are brilliant at passing babygear around on a network. Never be too proud to accept anything; it saves you an amazing amount of money.

Earache

Two of my children have suffered very badly from earache. One of them screamed all night and we had no idea what was the matter with him. At about four in the morning I figured it out by going all over him with my hand, pressing gently to see if doing it in any one place made him scream even louder. He did when I got to his ear. So, if a baby screams persistently even though it's dry, fed, winded, wee'd and poo'd and hasn't got a temperature, it may well have earache. If you press very gently with the flat of your hand over the whole ear and it screams even louder, you know it's got earache.

Older children will hold their ear obviously, so you can tell. At various times, depending on the seriousness of the pain, I've been successful with sitting the child upright with a hot water bottle over the ear, plus an infant painkiller – follow instructions exactly. If this doesn't work after a few hours then the doctor has to have a look, because the ear drum can burst and/or something ghastly called a mastoid infection can happen. The point is, if you can disperse the gunk in the ear without going to the doctor, you can avoid having to pump the child with antibiotics, or putting it through various kinds of mini-operation.

The reason why little children are afflicted with earaches is because children under seven have very narrow Eustachian tubes that can't always drain easily. Something went wrong in the design, apparently. If you've never tried homeopathy, then this is where you could start. Various homeopathic remedies will disperse mucus.

Eating Out

Unless you go to Macdonald's, the Happy Eater, and fish and chip shops, eating out with kids in England is often a nightmare. If you have fond memories of you and your partner enjoying nice leisurely meals in super little restaurants, then whatever you do, don't confuse those memories with what you will experience with one or more little ones in tow. Certain strategies are in order. I found that rather than try to coax my children to sit on a chair, it's easier to have any child under two on my knee. Waiting for food to come is always agony, and a few handy games like variations on I-spy, knock-knock and so on are useful.

All my children have always loved to go on sight-seeing tours to the toilets. 'I wanna go to the toilet, Dad', means 'I wanna check out the loo seats.'

Choose simple food, like baked potatoes, and be prepared to eat vast amounts of leftovers, especially of Knickerbocker Glories. Ignore snotty waiters and ask for extra bowls, plates, tea spoons and paper napkins so that all the necessary decanting, dividing up of quarter portions and wiping can take place. Get out before they go on further sight-seeing tours round all the other tables.

Stand by for the loud embarrassing comment announced to the whole restaurant: 'Dad, what's a foreskin?' Or loud singing of 'Happy birthday to you, I want to go to the loo, I want to do a poo', followed by hysterical giggling. Get a babysitter as soon as possible afterwards and go to your favourite restaurant to remind yourselves what it used to be like when you were young and carefree.

Eating out abroad can be tricky, especially in France where the gaps between the courses are longer than the courses themselves. As far as children are concerned this is pure hell. Why does it take half an hour from the time you've had cheese till the orange arrives? I remember on one occasion sitting next to a French family, and little Danielle was about two and wasn't allowed to leave her seat for the full two-hour stint. Every time she looked like she might slide off the edge of her chair, Dad stared at her and shouted, 'Danielle – je te parle!' Presumably this treatment, carried out regularly over several years, trains les petits français. When I tried saying 'Eddie, I'm speaking to you!' he said, 'Yeah, I know, I can hear you, Dad.'

Equality

There's one school of thought that says equality is a nasty idea invented by communists, impossible to achieve and disastrous however you attempt to put it into practice. This school proves its case by saying women can't be boxers because their breasts get in the way and plumbers can't be judges because they don't speak proper.

I'm not ashamed of it. This book is to do with trying to bring about a certain kind of equality. It's based on two ideas: one, that women are human beings; and two, that men are too.

If women are human beings then they're entitled to go out and do whatever men enjoy doing. If women go out and enjoy whatever men enjoy doing, *and* have babies, then someone has to share in the childcare. People with enough money hire nannies, though this still leaves the evenings and weekends. People without have to work it out somehow.

If fathers are human beings too, then one of the ways of proving it is by having something to do with those *other* human beings called children. Fathers who totally avoid childcare always seem to me to be trying to avoid paying their dues as members of the human race.

I'm under no illusion, as they say, that if every father took equal shares in childcare then 'equality' would have arrived. But certain possibilities would crop up: doing different kinds of work changes us. A woman not 100 per cent devoted to the needs of others becomes different. A man becoming in part devoted to the needs of others does too.

Feeding Babies

If you haven't already found out, you will very soon discover that your nipples don't seem to give a baby much of a treat. This means that your role in the first stages when your partner is breastfeeding is limited to such things as finding cushions to jam under partner's elbow, supplying gallons of liquids, not arguing when she says 'Breastfeeding is work, too, you know', answering the telephone, and generally keeping marauders away from the cave.

When or if the dreaded bottle arrives, then let's face it, there is no real reason why bottle filling, cleaning and giving should be a female task. After all, blokes don't seem to have much trouble topping up the oil, water and battery.

Obvious points:

1. Follow the instructions on the side of the tin, EXACTLY.
2. Be neurotically careful about keeping bottles and teats sterilized.

When you're feeding, head off to a room on your own without your partner, mother or mother-in-law – the first few times, the baby will be easily distracted by the smell and sound of mother; and anyway, you don't want to *feel* an incompetent nerd, even if you are one.

Hold the baby firmly in the crook of your stronger arm and focus your eyes on the baby's eyes. Making chooky-chooky noises is not some nutty thing that besets women in their dotage; it keeps the baby focusing, and gives it a sound cue to link with the food. So pluck up courage and make some reassuring noise, such as tongue clicking or a low burbling of the times-tables, accompanied by smiling and much eyebrow work.

Don't jam the bottle in like you're gardening or something; ease it in, and be prepared for the baby to be bored. If it is, wiggle the teat about a bit – remember, a very young baby is basically a mouth with a brain and body attached. Getting through a successful feed is a really nice feeling for the baby, and even better for you. You feel ultra-competent.

The baby will be sick. This may come just at the end of the feed, after an hour's hard work. Bloop! straight over the trousers. And the funny thing is, it always looks like more came out than went in. Now you have to decide whether to try again or leave it for a bit. Mostly, leave it for a bit, because even though it looks like more, it's actually less. Technically, this kind of bloop is really just a high velocity burp. Anyway, who cares *what* it is when your trousers are soaking with warm sicked-up milk? Therefore, come prepared with towel. Forget the PVC apron touch – bloop just pours off it, down your socks.

Panic for first-timers: the baby bloops several times. This happened to me with my first-born so I dashed for help to old Dr Spock and he talked about something where the stomach or gut grows together. PANIC! But then he pointed out that the baby would have to bloop *every* feed and be losing weight for this to be the problem.

See WINDING, WEANING AND GETTING ON TO SOLIDS

Feeding Toddlers

When you're about two or three, then there are loads more interesting things to do than sit around a table chewing: you could be under the table, on the table, sticking lego into the food, putting your finger up your nose, and so on. Remember, so long as a parent isn't stoking a child up with biscuits, sweets and ice-creams in between meals, then at some point or other hunger will get to it and it'll eat. No child will starve itself. The point about the biscuits etc. is serious: a child will quickly learn it can get away with dodging mealtimes *and* get a pound of biscuits at three o'clock. All my kids have tried this on, in their time. What's needed here is *firmness*.

Firmness in this case does not mean forcing a child to eat everything you've dished up and making every meal a battle-ground. It's tough to admit it, but you don't always know best about things like, say, whether a child is hungry or not. But it does mean being consistent: if you say there's nothing else to eat until tea-time . . . then stick to it. Let them know that what you cook is what there is. Don't get up and start cooking something else or they'll soon learn that one, too.

Be prepared to go in for jollying-up exercises. I do: 'here comes the helicopter [spoon heads for mouth] landing now [into mouth]'. And one of my children liked the fork-lift truck routine, with the little bird for variation. Do remember that their arms actually get tired reaching up to the table. If a bit of lap-sitting looks like it'll do the trick, then take it in turns with your partner from meal to meal so you're not having a barney about it.

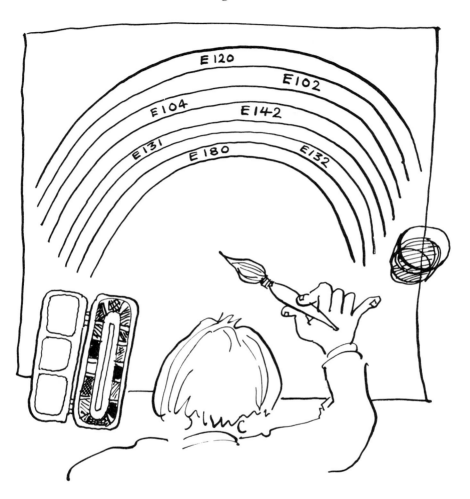

For children to enjoy eating, then mealtimes should be good times in a general sense. Three-year-olds go in for spontaneous singing and hours of knock-knock jokes that don't make sense: Knock-knock – who's there? – Potato – Potato who? – Carrots [hysterical laughter]. Four-year-olds turn their plates of food into film-sets and act out war movies, fairy stories and Japanese cartoons with the peas and gravy. Notice I've left two-year-olds out of this sequence. Two-year-olds are dangerous anarchists and would rather eat under the table or hanging from the lampshade – and often do. One reason for this *may* – and I mean only 'may' – be that you're unwittingly dosing them up with stimulants. Take time out to read the sides of packets of fish fingers, soft drinks and the like and figure out just how many additives you're pumping into your little loved one.

Back to serious things: anything with sugar in is, in its own way, addictive. In other words, once they've discovered the joys of the chocolate biscuit, or whatever, then they'll prefer that to a bit of fish, a tomato, or a carrot. If you are one of the two people in the world who enact a strict 'no sweets, biscuits, jelly, buns ever, ever, ever' routine, then you won't have a problem here and your children will happily munch raw carrots any time of day or night. If, like me and most people, you're a compromise person, and try to dish up fresh veg, salads, fresh fruit, and not too much tinned and frozen food and sweets, then you'll find yourself in the position of saying 'Just one bit of cabbage' or 'One leaf of lettuce, or there's no afters'. Once again, so long as you stick to what you've said on the day, and you stick to more or less the same line from day to day, then it'll work out.

One last do-or-die method I've used goes like this: 'Come on, eat up, it's really nice . . . you don't want it? . . . None of it? . . . OK, I'll eat it . . .' [I open mouth very wide and bring it near the plate, making growling noise]. Sometimes this works and they shout 'No, don't eat it, don't eat it, I'll eat it'. Sometimes they think it'll look really funny and they want to watch you gobble up the mashed-up gunk on their plate. Tough! You have to go through with it so that they know next time you really do mean that you'll eat it. That's what's hard about sticking to your line.

Be prepared to leave their food on the table for a bit, after everyone's finished. I can't think of the number of times my youngest has left a full plate, saying 'I don't want none of it!' and then come back to the table about twenty minutes later and wolfed down the lot.

First Night with Baby at Home

This is a strange and unnerving experience. I spent the whole night listening to him breathing. What would happen if he stopped? How would I know? Do newborn babies dream? Every little snuffle and squeak, I was wide-eyed and staring. I got up at least ten times just to go and look at him to check he was real. What if he's cold? What if he's too hot? Who is he, anyway?

The birth kept going round and round in my head. The very first sight of him. Is a baby a person? What if I'm a complete dead loss as a dad? How would I cope if there was something awful? Is he OK? What if he was Down's Syndrome and they hadn't spotted it? How would we know? What would I do if he was disabled? Would we cope? Will I earn enough money to keep him? Should we move out of the flat, since my flat-mate didn't reckon on this when he sub-let the place to me. Where shall we go? I hope his belly button heals up soon. Ah, he wants a feed. How long's that? Three hours. Must sleep, must sleep.

And all the while, you really can't believe that where before there were just two of you, now there are three. And that is an incredible feeling.

Food and Cooking

How will you be remembered by your children? As the one
who, when Mum wasn't there, dished up revolting food? I love
my Dad for many things, but when Mum went to evening
classes on Monday nights, he would smack his lips and say
'Lovely, cold meat for us tonight, boys.' And we hated it.
Chunks of cold, damp meat made Monday nights dreadnights.
Yet there was one dish he could make that we absolutely
adored. And just to make it taste even better, Mum said it was
bad for us. It was a Jewish dish called Matzo Brah (spelling
guessed) which involved soaking broken matzos (those large
water-biscuit-like things) in water, dunking them in beaten egg
and frying the bits in chicken fat. And when we had it he
would always say, 'Don't tell Connie I've given you Matzo
Brah.' The moral of this story I take to be, that it's not a bad idea
to have a few Dad's Specials up your sleeve. Learn what it is to
be loved for the food you cook, but get ready to duck if the
woman in your life feels undermined. Your line here is: 'But
darling, every meal I cook frees your mind.' Well, something
like that . . .

One of the most important techniques to get hold of is how to rustle together nice nosh very quickly. And this means nice nosh for everyone: the baby you're in charge of, your partner, friends, anyone drifting in. I've found that the best thing to do is have a repertoire of basics that you can play around with.

Starting with the youngest (see WEANING for first foods, and FEEDING TODDLERS), you want to have a range from emergency rations to extra specials. Emergency rations are things like peanut butter sandwiches, baked beans, fish fingers, bananas, yoghurt, toast fingers, cheddar cubes, tomato segments and cucumber slices. A screaming one-year-old can be silenced in minutes with this stuff, so always make sure you've got supplies handy. Don't use the gooey egg, it's not worth the salmonella risk.

Not so quick and easy are a range of things using cheese, tuna fish, beans, sweet corn, peas, green beans and chick peas, yesterday's boiled or baked potato. Any combination of these, grilled, usually goes down well. The problem with meat is that in convenience form – i.e. sausages, hamburgers and the like – a glance down the list of ingredients gives you much cause for thought, while fresh meat takes time to fetch, prepare and cook.

When it comes to preparing more elaborate things, spurn not the noble casserole and stew. Here you can junk together all your favourite foods and flavours, dish it up to everyone and have some left over for tomorrow to save you time then. I've found that sloppy rather than dry goes down best with younger ones. The cheap and quick way is to literally grab anything you like the taste of, chop it up into half-inch chunks, fling it in a big saucepan, top it up with water and simmer for two hours. Use some or any of the following: potatoes, tinned tomatoes, chick peas, kidney beans, onion, brown lentils, red lentils, carrots, barley, rice, cabbage, parsnip, broccoli, cauliflower, beef, lamb and chicken. For flavouring experiment with parsley, marjoram, garlic, stock cubes, bouillon cubes, mustard, lemon, tomato purée.

If you're looking for quick, tasty and good food, then you really can't beat Italian sauce and pasta. In fact, an Italian sauce is a great basis for loads of dishes. Quick simmer method: mash up tinned tomatoes with a potato masher, add tomato purée, garlic, basil, oregano, tarragon, thyme and lemon rind. Experiment with quantities of it. The minimum cooking time is about twenty-five minutes for the flavours to meld. This sauce you can use with pasta and grated cheese, or you can pour it on any kind of veg, or meat. Optional extras are green and red peppers, capers, mushrooms (see recipe book for the full olive oil number).

As for the pasta, go mad. Get every and any variety you can get. Here is a wonderful chance to give your children choice, food games and fun, and with really good food. My three-year-old and seven-year-old are both addicts. Whenever I say what do you want, they always say 'Pasta' and we go through the coils and bows and tubes and green ones and orange ones. I slop on the sauce with grated cheese, can't fail. Tinned pesto is another winner; dilute it with water rather than olive oil so it isn't too rich, stir it into the hot pasta and add grated cheese.

Rice is another winner especially if you experiment with different kinds of rice: round grain, long grain, white, brown, patna.

Any leftover veg or frozen packets or rice can all be stir-fried. Note: olive oil tastes best: buy the most expensive, extra virgin; use tiny quantities; and get it hot before you add the veg or rice.

Dishing up food can be a wonderful and satisfying business that makes you feel very wanted and loved, but it can also be a heartless and thankless task. Stand by for abuse, sulking, and fussiness. The line 'this is what I've cooked, I haven't cooked anything else' is a vital weapon in your armoury, to which you add 'and you're not pigging out on biscuits instead'. Compromises can be reached over a little bit of picking out of 'bits I don't like, dad'. Not too much, or you'll go crazy. Your general aim is to go for enjoyable but healthy. Try to avoid the usual dad's easy option technique, which is mum cooks but I dish up convenience food. If you do this, you undermine partner's life and child's stomach.

Getting Away

You're each entitled to equal time away from the struggle. If you want to go to an evening class on electric guitar, then your partner is entitled to go swimming the following night. If you think you want to spend a week walking in the Peak District, then your partner is entitled to a week somewhere too. It may never be exactly fair swops, but it should be roughly so, otherwise resentment rears its ugly head. Let's say you both work, and one thing you say you need to do after work is go round to the pub for a packet of crisps and a drink. This is Getting Away. If you participate in or follow a sport, this too is Getting Away. And if it is classifiable as Getting Away, your partner is entitled to equal quantities of it. My going to watch Arsenal on Saturdays equals my wife's swimming lessons.

So far, so simple. Here come the complications: what one person says is Work, the other person might say is Getting Away. Or even worse, what one person says is Work, the other person might say is Not-work. So, if you are both agreed you want children, then getting in money to pay for the household is Work. But then, maintaining the household and childcare are also Work. To illustrate these complications: 'Sorry, love, I had to go off for a drink after work, there was quite a lot of stuff to tie up for tomorrow.' (This could be fibs.) 'While you've been in the pub, I've been getting the tea. I'm going out now, see you!'

By and large, so far in the history of the world, blokes seem to have learnt the tricks of this game much better than women. Sorting out a bit of EQUALITY in these matters may do wonders for your love-life. Women report that sex with a bloke they think is exploiting them is either impossible or unpleasant.

Goodbyes

You can't avoid these. As some children get older, they get more and more unhappy about goodbyes. The problem with knowing more about the world is that you also know more about awful things that could happen to your parents. They could sink with the *Titanic*, drown in a river, turn into a ghost, or whatever. They know it's possible, they've seen it in books, on telly and maybe heard about friends or relations. So goodbyes can get more difficult not less, especially round the age of three or four.

I once saw Sheila Kitzinger handing out a bit of advice on this. She said, why don't you give the child you're saying goodbye to something 'very important' to look after: like a special key ring, or an old bank card. Tell them they've got to look after it until you get back.

I've tried this and it is a great help, especially if you make a fuss about it when you get back, or in the morning if it's when a babysitter comes. In fact, shortly before I wrote this I had The Cling treatment from my three-year-old when I dropped him off at nursery school. Some of the children were painting daffodils, so with him clinging on to my leg I painted a daffodil, one of the nursery teachers hung it up to dry and I said to him: 'Look after my daffodil, won't you? Make sure no one spoils it, so when I come to pick you up I can take it home.' He seemed appeased.

Smaller children can be convinced by cheque books, diaries, watches and the like, but you have to play it for real from start to finish.

Hairwashing

This is one of the great childhood terrors. And they're often afraid of it even before they've experienced shampoo in the eye and water up the nose. Having experienced it, they turn wild. For this I've needed soundproof ears, gritty determination, a firm hand and a good line in bad jokes and jollification. Knock knock – Who's there? Boo – Boo who? – No need to cry about it ... Mmm, well, it's the way you tell it.

Try any or all of the following techniques. I cannot guarantee success; they have at times nearly worked for me, but you will not get your money back if they fail. Never use adult shampoo; give the child a flannel to put over its eyes; buy one of those brims without a crown; let them feel the water in the jug before you tip it on; hold their head back so the water can't go in their eyes, telling them to hold on to the side of the bath.

I've figured out that the screaming is actually therapeutic. It gives them something to focus on while you do the dirty deed. It's worth explaining to your neighbours what the cause of the noise is: invite them in if they don't look like they believe you. They will never come again.

Health Visitor

In the first days and then at various times in the first year, a health visitor will call. It's a slightly ambiguous moment because they come both to help you and to see if you are treating the baby properly. This means that you may feel you're being snooped on. No matter how nice they are, no matter how they appear to be looking at the baby, they are also making judgements about you.

On one occasion I found myself feeling guilty about the dirty washing-up and then getting irritated by the fact that really the health visitor wanted to see my wife and not me. The point is, they don't really expect to see a man on his own looking after a baby, so if you're in this situation, stand by for one or two little awkwardnesses. One reason may be that the visitor is on the lookout for POST-NATAL DEPRESSION and is suspicious about why the mother isn't there.

If you're an evenings and weekends dad, then the health visitor will be no more than a name.

Helplessness

This is a skill learned at an early age by most men when faced with dirty washing, an empty fridge, a splinter in a thumb, or a screaming younger brother. This develops very neatly into helplessness in parenthood when faced with a pooey nappy, a wet babygrow, an empty fridge, a splinter in a child's thumb, or a screaming nipper.

If this book has any purpose at all, it is to undermine this sense of helplessness. Yet, even as I say that, I can't help admitting that helplessness isn't all bad. Even when we are capable, we still get bouts of helplessness. I've been defeated by buggies that won't fold, lost keys, sleepless babies, car break-downs, diarrhoea (child's, not mine), a bad back (mine, not child's), and rain. In fact, one of the tricks of the fatherhood game is to forego the need to achieve and be a winner. You can admit that some days you feel helpless. Some days you only managed to do one thing: buy some orange juice. Some days all you did was potter about doing nothing and so nothing was achieved . . . and that's OK.

A shady side of helplessness is that you may notice some women are sometimes glad that you feel helpless. It works like this: women were told to do the domestic stuff and childcare. They got good at it. They were proud they were good at it. Then along comes a man and has a go at it and he's not as good at it as they are – or at least, they hope he isn't. Men then think, oh well, they're right, I'm not really much good at it, I'll go down the pub. And we're right back to square one.

Holidays

I was once in the middle of shooting a TV film and the lighting man was showing his family album. Some of the pictures were of him and his children on the beach about fifteen years earlier, when they were toddlers. He looked at them and said, 'You know, when I look at these, there's one thing that bothers me. When I remember that holiday, all I can remember is shouting at the kids for being naughty, but look at them. Look how small they are.'

It doesn't matter how often I think of that conversation, I still know that on holiday there's even more chance of my getting ratty and shouting than at any other time. Why is this? I think one of the reasons must be that, no matter how hard I try, on holiday I always end up thinking about holidays I had when I didn't have children, and I climbed mountains or hitched across France. It's good old boring male egotism. And yes, holidays are potential disaster areas.

The first rule of holidays is that the nicer the place, the more horrible the journey (see CAR JOURNEYS). It's always your flight that sits on the runway for an hour with the air-con switched off. It's only your children that are screaming in the departure lounge. It's only your children that people are praying they won't have to sit next to.

Once there, you face the hard, cruel reality of what shared childcare means when you've got no excuse to nip off to work, phone your friend or see that crucial football match. Will you have the stamina to play dot to dots, build sand castles, and go and see the donkey for the hundredth time?

The problem is that holidays with children have to be family-shaped. It's no use trying to squeeze a baby and a two-year-old into a wild outdoor adventure, or a chic rave. The problem with family-shaped holidays is that they can be boring. In the circumstances, as my wife has to remind me every single holiday, it is grossly unfair on the children to complain to them about it.

I fear I have made holidays sound terrible. They're not. Amazing and wonderful moments can happen. And the best way for them to happen is through not trying. Little children like holidays to be in safe places where they can play about near you and they're not constantly being carted off to see the next fascinating tree, wall, holy fountain, or Olde Inne. Some of the most exciting cave paintings in Europe are in the Pyrenees. My two-year-old's response to these was to fall asleep in my arms, and so for one hour's worth of stooping and bending in the dark I carried him fast asleep past the bison, the deer, the stags and the rest.

The best holidays my children have had have been where there's been a swimming pool, young ones included. I find it difficult to stay in the water longer than four hours at a time, but they don't understand how I can give up so soon. Other highlights: castles, beaches, donkeys, sheep, old-fashioned sweet shops, blackberry picking and ice-cream parlours. Turn-offs: bookshops, churches, Indian restaurants, heat, flies and guides with loud voices.

See EATING OUT

Hugging and Kissing

I'm told some men feel a bit funny about this, especially with boy children. I have to say I find babies very huggable and squeezable. If you don't there isn't anything worse than seeing other people going goo goo, squeeze squeeze all over the place. It seems so phoney. I think the more of the muck and crap you get involved with, the easier it is to feel huggish towards babies. Once you've got into hugging your babies, then there never seems to be any reason why you should stop. As I say elsewhere, my fourteen-year-old hulk still wants cuddles.

Mind you, if you really aren't a hugger then kids are pretty good at spotting the phoney hug. On the other hand, even if you haven't been one, you might find you can grow to like it. Intriguingly, some children are more into it than others. Some like to flop out on your lap and tuck their head into your neck, and give you squeezes, while others keep their distance. You have to respect that.

Mine go in for a mock-up of a demanding-brat routine to disguise the fact that they are – well – demanding brats. It all started with my ten-year-old. At any time between the age of two and eight he would go in for a kind of droopy wail: 'Da-a-a-d, ca-a-a-an I sit on yoooou? D-a-a-a-d, sta-a-a-a-y with meeeee. Da-a-a-ad, uppy, uppy', and so on. The only way I could cope was to give him the cuddle but to repeat the 'D-a-a-a-a-d' wail at the same time. This caught on, and now whenever anyone wants a cuddle in our house, they give it the intro of 'D-a-a-a-a-a-d'.

Indoor-itis

This can strike any child under ten after spending too long indoors. The over-tens just get sulky and eat biscuits. Under-tens' symptoms of indoor-itis to look out for are repeated banging of head up and down on sofa, getting into small dark corner of the house and jumping up and down on brother, sister, cousin or friend, heaving on your neck, kicking the skirting board.

Eddie is the main indoor-itis sufferer in our house, so we bought him a 'PT bouncer'. This is a very small trampoline. Every time Eddie starts showing any of the symptoms (normally with him it's all of them at the same time), we shout: 'Eddie – bouncer!' and he heads off and bangs out about a thousand or so leaps.

Other cures for indoor-itis: house-dwellers – open back door, apply short but firm pressure on child's shoulders in direction of open door, count three, close door; flat-owners – hard luck, it's the park, or yet another trip counting paving stones and red cars. I notice that, traditionally, these trips seem to have been designated as Dads' Jobs. Standing in a park on a Sunday afternoon you would think the nation was jammed full of single fathers. I always imagine that this is a consequence of the same little scene played out in millions of houses all over the country just after lunch:

HER: Ooh, it's nice to put your feet up after lunch.
HIM: Yeah, really nice.
KID 1: Park park park park park.

HIM: Hear that, love? She's pretending to be the dog. What's on the telly?

HER: She's saying 'park' with a 'p'.

HIM: Uh-huh.

KID 2: Park park park park.

HER: Ooh, it's nice to put your feet up after lunch.

HIM: I agree.

HER: Shame you can't fit it in this afternoon.

KID 1 AND KID 2: Park park park park park park ... (*until dad grabs football, kite and Sunday newspaper and stumps off with kids*)

HER: Oooh, it's nice to put your ...

HIM: (*leaving*) All right, I heard, I heard.

Jealousy

It's something I've always been reluctant to admit, but there's a very good chance that you will feel jealous of babies and children. I tell myself that it's OK to be jealous but it's not OK if I pretend I'm not, because otherwise it'll come out in some other mean and nasty way. Basically, right from the start, if your partner is breastfeeding this can, deep down, be a big disappointment. Here was this part of my partner that both of us seemed to think me fondling was a good idea. Possibly I told myself that in some way or another it belonged to me. Not in reality, of course, but I had noticed that whereas my partner was quite happy to offer her hand to friends and strangers, she didn't do the same thing with her chest. It seemed like I was in some sort of privileged situation, here. And then along comes the baby, and the little creature has total and unlimited access. And it's not just any old access – it adores it, it gurgles at it, it falls asleep on it, it squeezes it, it devours it. I've been elbowed out.

It's worth putting in a bit of time thinking about this. Find out if deep down you do actually feel fed up about it. If you do, let it out. I've made jokes about it to help me admit what was going on: 'Hey, what are you doing, little one? I thought that was mine!' Meanwhile I've had to face up to some hard truths: my partner's body isn't mine – any of it. If I want my child to be confident and happy then lots of breastfeeding willingly given is a great boost. And there's something else: when finally the weaning takes place, my loved one's nipples may be about as sensitive as boiled cabbage. This may disappoint her but the great feminist guru, Sheila Kitzinger herself, recommends frequent friendly stroking and squeezing. Yippee!

In a rather Freudian way, I've reduced jealousy merely to your partner's breasts (the psychological justification being that it reminds you unconsciously of the time your own mother put away her breasts and seemed to be spending too much time with your father). Obviously, jealousy can hang around in all sorts of places. I am not saying anything dangerously new in noting that some women, especially in relationships where the loving element has gone into decline (or is it *because* it's gone into decline?) put all their affections onto the children, especially a boy. The standard line in situations like this is to blame the woman. Before you leap to curse your partner for giving all her love to the little brat, consider that you might just possibly be partly responsible for the situation. You letting childcare be carried out solely by your partner is her reason for devoting herself to the children, which is in turn your reason for having your nose out of joint. In other words, this whole business of taking over chores traditionally done by women has repercussions that go quite deep. There is the possibility that some traditional resentments can be relieved.

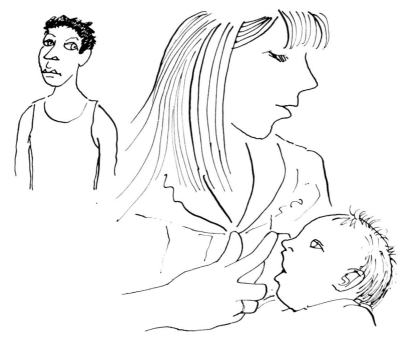

Kids' Cooking

I'm not talking here of older children flinging hamburgers about and begging to make chocolate cookies and honeycomb toffee all Sunday. No, this is the story of the little fingers in the pizza dough and the jam tart. There's no question, small children feel wonderful being part of making food. It may drive you crazy, because you thought you were going to bash out those pizzas in half an hour because you wanted to watch the football. No chance. 'Can I help?' says your two-and-a-half-year-old.

One trick here if you really don't want to take five hours to make those damn pizzas is to privatize your pizzas and give him his own little pizza to make. And remember: his will be the one that tastes the best, and everyone has to clap his pizza.

If you're a dab hand at cakes and so on, then the real interest will be the opportunity to lick the bowl. This is all very well, but maybe you want to lick it yourself. Children are also very good at greasing pans and mashing tinned tomatoes. Wear goggles.

Little Chauvy Pigs

Little boys sometimes go in for being horrible to mum. Freud claimed to know why, but the question for men is what do we do about it? If we dive in as the heavy dad: 'How dare you throw toast at your mother?', all it does is reinforce the idea that men are tough and women feeble. If we do nothing it gives the message you agree that being beastly to mum is a good idea. I suggest the following:

1. When mum's not around you give the little lad an earful about why you don't like these goings on. This avoids upstaging mum.
2. You have an interesting conversation with your partner (!) where in an instantaneous flash of understanding you both come to the conclusion that at the actual moment of the boy's beastliness it's down to her to say 'No, I don't want you to blow raspberries in my face', 'No, I won't get your cornflakes if you yell at me', but *you* will do the support business when you've got the blighter on his own.

P.S. If Freud was right, remember the reason for the beastliness is because he's fed up that mum sleeps with you and/or has had another child.

Middle-Class Curriculum

Whatever the pros and cons of the National Curriculum, it seems to me it has sharpened up the whole question of how parents supplement their children's education. Perhaps all that schools do is confirm children's parents' status, education and ambition. A friend of mine was rather wearily lugging his daughter from a piano class to a computer workshop one Sunday when he looked out of his car window and said: 'I'm just doing the middle-class curriculum.'

I'm sure most people reading this book will know of children who are rushed from piano lessons to swimming lessons then on to theatre club on Fridays, art class on Saturday mornings, dance on Sunday mornings and so on . . . The process used to be restricted to the seven and overs but I notice it's got a hold on the five and unders and now there are singing classes for one-year-olds and poetry classes for two-year-olds and gymnastics for three-year-olds, and the whole thing is matched by hundreds of books guiding you in how to make your child a neurotic – sorry, I mean a high achieving – credit to your skills as a parent.

I can't think of anything more dreary than seeing and hearing tired little children screeching away hatefully on violins, and cursing cold swimming pool water. Somehow you have to juggle with following children's real enthusiasms, putting opportunities in front of them they would otherwise not have, being prepared to drop things when the child is uninterested, helping them achieve things for their own satisfaction rather than yours and the neighbours'. My present fourteen-year-old has never really bitten on any of the things

I've put his way: photography, computers, foreign travel, swimming, football, poetry. On the other hand, he's really taken off on something that I know nothing about, couldn't help him with if I tried, and never see him do: skateboarding. With skateboarding, I guess he feels under no pressure from me, his mother or school. It's totally self-led.

If I were to be balanced about this, then I should be pointing out here the difference between the kind of pressure-cooking I've described and the matter of 'giving opportunities' and 'introducing experiences'. Somehow or another we have to do this without it being a burden to our children, as in 'let's go and look at this old church, it's got a fifteenth-century nave and fourteenth-century font, you know . . .' With very young children, the most important opportunities we give them are space, time, and attention. Rushing them hither and thither dumping them into stimulating classes seems to make them panicky or blasé. This I know from comparing the children I do performances for (it's a kind of one-man show): the most difficult ones to handle are the Sunday morning Arts Centre ones where the super little darlings appear to know it all. In fact, the only time I've ever had my face spat in was by a super little darling.

At home, young children need corners or rooms where they are safe, little chairs and tables, plenty of paints, paper, things to model with (clay, plasticine, play-dough), cardboard boxes, glue, scissors, plenty of books, story-tapes, music-tapes, things to bang and blow, dressing-up boxes and cast-off home items like old telephones, saucepans and the like. With all these things, in conjunction with time, space and attention, they will make more opportunities happen for themselves than you or I can imagine.

Minders

This can be nightmare or bliss. A brief talk with friends will reveal the full range, from over-worked ratty old biddies who plonk the children down in a roomful of potties, toys, televisions and sweets and leave them all day, to brilliant intuitive infant teachers who take them for walks and visits, and find new and interesting things for them to do.

Remember, you are only paying for a minder, not a Suzuki teacher. The abysmal under-5s childcare situation in this country means that nearly everybody suffers: parents, children and minders. Nearly all parties can come out of the situation feeling aggrieved.

So, how to choose a minder? If it's you that's doing some of the ferrying to and fro, then make sure the minder is someone who can cope with a man and isn't overcome with embarrassment every time she sees you. When you're checking out the situation, you need to look at the state of toys, safety of heaters and windows, what kind of food she dishes up, how many children, whether she takes them out, if so, where and why and how does she look after all the children on the roads, is she in a reasonably contented state of mind and not in some lousy relationship where she's being hit or is hitting the bottle.

Of course all this involves scrutiny, and scrutiny can be resented. It's part of the vicious circle of everyone checking out everyone else. You might find, as a man, that this feels like female biz and you retreat in the face of it. Understandable, but if you do, then you have to accept that this gives off very specific messages to your child: 'Dad isn't interested in my life at the minder's . . .'

My partner hatched out a plan with some friends that was something of an improvement. Three households employed two women to look after our children for varying lengths of time in our houses. We advertised for the women, paid them over the rate and during holidays, and we also provided food for the children. About once every six months there was a meeting between people from the three households to discuss things like people dropping out, pay increases, illnesses and so forth. It seemed like one of the best arrangements that I've heard of.

Movement

Most of the baby manuals have nice little charts explaining the stages a baby goes through, hands waving, head lifting, back arching and so on. It can be really nice watching all this. I mean, before I had a baby, I thought babies were little immobile blobs that smelled. I had no idea that right from the start you can see expressions, movements and personality. More than that, there are times early on when you can see changes every day in these movements. This is wonderful.

Several things made an impact on me. If you get to sit with your baby right from the start, watch how it will scan your face. It may feel prattish, but use your face, and your eyes especially, and talk and sing to the baby. Don't worry about what nutty and gooey things come out of your mouth. You'll be amazed how soon the baby starts recognizing you. I nod and stroke the baby's cheek with the back of my finger. Watch out here for the milk reflex, when the baby turns to face the thing tickling her cheek because she thinks it's a nipple.

One of the first things my first wife's mother made us do, after we had bathed our first boy, was to lie him down on his back in front of the fire with just his top on, to let him kick. Then for about five minutes or so, he kicked his little legs. He seemed to love it and my mother-in-law said it would strengthen his legs and back. It was a nice social time, too, when we could all sit round and enjoy the baby.

I once saw a film on TV of a three-month-old baby which aimed to show how babies communicate. They showed how it kept repeating certain gestures. These gestures seemed to be the same for one kind of situation, like wanting something to eat, or wanting to be picked up. The film repeated these situations in rapid sequence, whereupon you saw twenty repetitions of exactly the same gesture by the baby. In other words, what seemed like the slightly chaotic waving we think babies do, in fact had a clear pattern. It was yet more evidence that babies are not blobs. I then went away full of this to watch my little ones and any others I came into contact with and – yes – it worked. Only the other day, I looked into the pram at a friend's baby, and first I saw it read my face and then it made a repeated little move with one arm, then with the other, and a little turn of the head. It was instantly recognizable as a kind of 'hallo'.

For me, the biggest buzz in this area is getting the first smiles. All sorts of things make a baby smile. By the way, some very early smiling, first week or so, isn't actually smiling, it's a bit of grunting to go with nappy-filling. But after a couple of months or so, all sorts of things can make a baby smile, or even better, laugh: making popping noises, little raspberries, nodding and singing, swinging the baby up and down, jigging and singing, squeezing, blowing down her neck, burying your nose in his chest, twiddling your fingers, doing ventriloquist acts with a teddy or dolly. I really got into this, and have spent hours at it. It may sound weird, but being able to make a baby smile and giggle is one of the major achievements I've chalked up in my life.

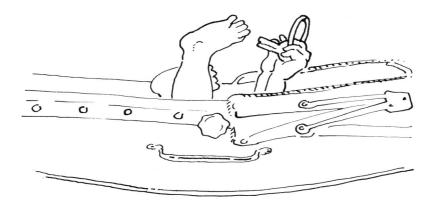

Nappies

There are probably quite deep reasons why, for some men, nappies represent the last threshold, the one you just cannot bear to cross. Yes, I'll do the shopping, the washing, the cooking, but nappies – no. What is being said here? That handling poo is one of those things with a female label on it? That those same human beings we think look great in those new clothes and smell wonderful in that perfume are also the best at nappies? Perhaps you feel a sense of panic even as you read this. If so, let me say this: first and foremost, getting a baby clean and fresh and dry is a nice thing to do. And if you move in quickly before the mess has had time to oxidize in the air, it doesn't actually smell too bad.

I had a rude awakening to the business long before I had children. My girlfriend at the time was in with a group of women who had decided to play a practical joke on their men. We went over to see a couple and their baby. When we got there, there were two other couples visiting. There was a bit of talking and suddenly I noticed that all the women had gone: there were four men and a baby – as in the film, plus one. We chatted on about football and other manly things for five minutes, ten, twenty, thirty and of course soon the baby started crying. There should have been a camera. We didn't know what to do, who was going to pick it up, who was going to jig it up and down, who was going to see if its nappy needed changing, who was going to do the nappy. In the end all four of us did it. There were eight hands on that baby, pushing and prodding and squeezing, trying to get it right. The whole thing had been a wicked conspiracy on the part of the mother to try and get her bloke to wise up. And this was in the days of . . . the Terry Towelling Nappy.

I guess that nearly everyone reading this will be spared the delights of shaking turds off terry nappies, and seeing stinking buckets of pissy ones standing in the bath. Such pleasures are gone. There really is no mystery about paper nappies, no magic folding tricks, no cunning deals with safety pins. I almost regret that my terry-nappy knowledge is redundant.

If you don't get in on nappies at the beginning, you never will. If you never do nappies, then your child will never see you as someone who deals with the real, basic stuff. Probably most men today are people who were brought up sharing constipation, sore foreskins, funny-coloured wee, itchy bums and the like only with their mothers. This may sound nutty, but I feel really good when I think that my kids have thought that dad as well as mum was a right person to help solve such problems. I was there with the salt water when the sore willy had to be dangled in. I was there teaching them how to wipe bums, and even as I'm writing this, I'm popping out of the room every so often to help my step-daughter massage her belly to help with constipation. All this kind of contact starts with nappies.

What is there to be said about paper nappies? My big mistake is always to yank the tabs too hard, so destroying the nappy in half a second. Over a year this can be an expensive mistake. If you put them on too tight it leads to rashes round the waist, and if they're too loose they leak. If you're confused by the mysticism of the ads, what they are basically saying is that 1. wee next to a baby's skin causes nappy rash; 2. our nappies hold loads of wee; 3. but don't panic because the brilliant way in which we make our nappies keeps the wee away from the skin. If you believe all they say about running shoes, you'll believe this too.

In other words, beware nappy rash. Everybody's life becomes hell when nappy rash is around. Small wonder; I don't suppose I'd keep very quiet if the whole of my bum was stinging all day. You only had to show a paper nappy to my second child and his bum would look like a tomato. What to do? The best and most impractical cure for nappy rash is the no-nappy treatment. If you expose most nappy rashes to the air, they go. But of course this also exposes your carpets to wee. This is where you rediscover the prehistoric virtues of the terry nappy. You can lie a baby on them, you can pin them loosely on the child, you can mop up pools with them.

You can buy various ointments that claim to cure nappy rash. The problem here is that they may or may not work, assuming that the newly ointmented surface is not going to get drenched with urine every hour on the hour. In other words, you may need both ointment and the fresh air treatment.

Once cured, you may have to go for the barrier method. Basically this is like fitting a damp course to your house. The old method here is reliable but slow and messy: vaseline. Vaseline makes a great wee-proof layer but when it's at room temperature it can be very stiff and hell to get off your hands. If you leave it on a radiator it'll soften, but then of course you may not be changing the baby near the radiator . . . Less efficient but easier to use and easier to clean off your hands are various zinc oxide creams. Take your choice.

Finally, where to do nappy changing? Much favoured is the changing-mat. It seems at first glance to solve all problems: the offending articles – the pissy pooey child and the pissy pooey nappy – are at arm's length, and any sudden explosions or fountains mostly land on the changing-mat's cleanable surface. So far, so good. But you will soon learn that fountains landing on the changing-mat are not absorbed, but run in rivulets towards the carpet, or much more likely, straight onto the clean vest and jumper. In other words, you need a changing-mat AND a terry nappy to put under the baby.

The other problem with the changing-mat method is the wriggle. As the baby gets older, the more it wriggles. My second child was not just a wriggler, he was a wrestler. It's at times like these you realize you don't have three arms and your head isn't much good at sticking down nappy tabs. Nappy-changing time becomes a time for much shouting, and skilful use of judo holds.

My solution to these changing-mat problems is to put the child over my knees. This way you can hold him down with the same arm that has the hand doing the nappy changing. With a terry nappy over your knees you can catch some of the fountain before it reaches your trousers, and you soon learn a quick upward hoist of the child to make sure you don't get soaked. Women seem generally to disapprove of changing nappies on knees, but it's nice to have individual and freaky ways of doing things. It makes you feel less slavish. With this over-the-knee technique, look out for the flailing feet. The child will learn very soon that as you sit there concentrating hard on wiping and tab-sticking, your chin is getting invitingly near. One kick of that lovely little pink foot and you're reeling. And they love it – cue for giggles and cackles and woman experts sitting around nodding, 'I told you so, I told you so.'

Changing nappies brings you into close contact with every digestive quirk. Even though you may never learn to spell it, diarrhoea becomes immensely important in your life. You discover such interesting facts as that babies on breast-milk only produce a not unpleasant mustard-coloured putty. You will be shocked to find that sometimes this isn't mustard-coloured, but bright green. Do not be alarmed: that's what it does when it hits oxygen. You will discover what babies can digest and what they can't. Sweet corn and raisins will never seem the same again, and the seed distribution systems of tomatoes and the like will become instantly clear to you. To revert to nappy rash – it's not always wee that causes the problem; in my experience, the thing is often triggered off by you being lazy about changing a pooey nappy. You think, OK, leave it just while I finish this cup of tea . . . three minutes . . . five minutes . . . and the damage has been done. It looks OK when you get round to changing it (after seven minutes), but by the time you get to the next nappy, there's the great red raw mess and the uncomprehending, pained eyes looking at you accusingly through the tears: why is my bum burning?

Now for a problem: changing nappies when you're out and about. Notice that motorway service stations have changing facilities in the ladies' loo only. Hard luck if you're on your own, it's the awkward sitting-on-the-loo job. If you're out on your own in other places, watch out for sympathetic old people who are probably thinking that your wife's just died; notice how all your men friends run like crazy at the sight of a baby's bum; observe parents and in-laws tut-tutting and unsure whether you should be doing this at all. Be brave, be bold, do it!

Nursery and Reception Class

This is about as far as this book takes you, up to the door of the first day of real school. It's at this moment you will remember The Cling (see SHAMING UP). What strategy will you use to ensure that your child doesn't hang on to you like a limpet, wailing pitifully? How will you ensure that this day is not indelibly marked in your child's brain as the day you deserted her and left her helpless in the control of totalitarian torturers?

Everyone is wondering this, and everyone is eyeballing everyone else, wondering which kid is going to crack first. Here's my solution: make for the sand-tray and get digging. Don't wait for your kid to go there. Just get over there and stuck in like it's the best thing that's happened since the ice cap retreated. Soon you will have a little cluster of kids around you. 'Hey, this looks good.' 'Yeah, I'm going to bury my Dad in here', says one cheery little girl.

Out of the corner of your eye, you notice that your own little dear is coming over too. Keep digging, muttering about how there's a lot of work to be done here. Other parents may now have run away and left their children in the capable hands of the totalitarian torturer and you. A few other parents are enwrapped in The Cling but trying to find an interesting book. The torturer will probably want to throw you out after a certain time. Pretend that your work in the sand-tray is nearing completion, but it's OK for the others to finish it off. Then quickly mutter to your own child, 'See you in a minute', and get out fast.

If you win this round, the rest is plain sailing till your child enters college, where you have to repeat the routine with the gas-ring in the student Hall of Residence.

Older Kids Attacking Baby

It's true, they do. You turn your back and POKE! In goes a finger and the little tiny thing is screaming. Sometimes they go in for leaving dangerous things in the cot, like a fully-armed Action Man. I shouldn't jest: my older one left a polythene bag in his baby brother's cot with malice aforethought. Beware of the over-keen hugger. 'Dad, let me hold the baby', and a little cuddle turns into a big juicy hug which turns into a half-nelson.

It's all understandable, if alarming. The older child has had you all for himself for the first months and years of his life and then along comes this screaming, sucking monster that every-one comes round to see and pat and hold and go goo-goo-goo at. If friends do come round, insist that they bring something for the older child. If it's couples coming, make them take it in turns to play with the older child. Tell them to avoid bright breezy gaffes like: 'Well, your baby sister looks terrific, I bet you're pleased, aren't you?' and 'Aren't you a lucky little chap to have such a beautiful little girl?' or 'Mum's busy, isn't she?'

The conventional role of the caring, considerate father in this circumstance has often been to take the older child on long loving outings to the zoo. This is probably a mistake. From his point of view, such outings mean: 'Ah, so Mum doesn't love me any more, she only loves the monster. And to prove it, you've wheeled me out of the house so she can get on with all that hugging and kissing with the monster. You're ganging up on me.'

The alternative is that you get stuck in with the new one and let the older one have some good times with mum, when she can reassure him he's a fantastic fellow and she still loves him.

On the Move

Some of the most hairy outings I've gone in for with children have been taking a child with me when I've been doing my show in a school. How did I manage the train journeys to places like Nottingham, taking my books, preparing for a performance, talking to the children and teachers afterwards and then travelling back on the train? All with a one-year-old in tow. In one school, when Eddie was about two, he refused to go into the nursery and so he sat at the side of the stage while I did the show. After about twenty minutes he got up and slowly started to crawl across the stage behind me. I just let him carry on, but then, just as slowly, the head of English in the school got up on the stage and started crawling after him. So there I was in the middle of trying to put something across to two hundred or so children, being upstaged by a baby and the head of English creeping about behind me.

Presumably you won't be quite as daft as I was, but there'll still be times when it's just you, the baby and the outside world. The most important item here is The Bag. If you're lazy and only in on this business as an auxiliary, you will let your partner do The Bag. She will say: 'She needs a drink, here's a change of track suit bottoms, I've put a knife in to peel the apple', and so on. This is all very comforting, but kind of debilitating. I've been like that with my third (our fifth) and it always seems like a reflection on my competence. You may not be so bothered.

What feels best is having your own Bag. You have your own supplies of stuff: terry nappies, baby lotion, vaseline, baby wipes, disposable nappies and so on, just as you have your

own toilet bag if you go away. You then also stuff in changes of clothes, two books (for the child, not you) that can be spun out in case of rained-off outings, long bus trips and the like, and always always always supplies of food and drink. Make sure the drink is really thirst-quenching and not just some sweet sticky thing, and the food is immediately consumable: sealed tubs of baby gunk or yoghurt with spoon, peanut butter sandwiches or whatever. Don't forget three polythene bags for putting nappies in in case you have to bring them home with you, and also for catching sick on board a bus. If there's room, maybe you can squeeze in a comfort toy and an engrossing toy. Lightweight rain gear goes in there too, because it's always too windy and it always rains. Changing-mat users will need a changing-mat.

The Bag itself should either be a rucksack or a shoulder bag, so that you can use two hands to carry the toddler and push the buggy. I used to use a bag that I slung across me so that I could carry him on one hip, the bag on the other. This allowed me to grope in the bag while still carrying the little fellow. The bag itself will need to be washable as it soon gets to smell of old food that you didn't empty out, wee, sick, sour milk and baby lotion. Lovely.

There are two very real dangers about the weather. Babies dehydrate in the hot weather and suffer from hypothermia in the cold, very, very easily. The explanation for this is down to the ratio of a baby's surface area to its overall body weight. Basically, it's as if they've got loads more skin than we have, and so they lose heat and/or water through their skin very much more quickly than an adult. In cold weather, a baby with an exposed head, neck, hands and feet is at risk. In very hot weather, you have to keep pumping in the fluids. The problem with both situations is that babies don't always shout about it to let you know they're suffering. If a baby isn't kept dry when it rains, it loses body heat very quickly straight through the clothes, and gets to a point where it is just as if it were naked. In an emergency, caught out in the rain, shove the baby under your coat, or better still, next to your skin.

Other Guys

It's no use pretending otherwise, being a share-care father can be a bit lonely. There aren't many other men doing it, and whereas women seem prepared to mix with other women on the sole basis that they are mothers, I for one have found it difficult to become friends with a man simply because he's a father. That probably says quite a lot either about me or about men in general. There's no question: in an ideal world, we would be able to behave towards each other in the way that mothers manage, giving each other advice and help on how to cope with teething, nappy rash and sleepless nights. Instead, these kinds of conversation we have with women. I can remember times when it's been me, my young child, a friend and his child, and we've sat and talked about everything *except* the children. It's almost as if we'd been saying to each other: 'Hey, look, we cope with this upbringing game without going in for long boring conversations about the best kind of shampoo, don't we?' Perhaps there's a sheepishness factor to overcome. Or perhaps men aren't very good at doing baby-talk: 'that's a nice babygrow your little girl's got . . .'

So, rather than set up fathers' outings, picnics, play-ins, etc. I've tended just to muck along with the playgroups and outings that local mothers have organized, or just go solo. You may not have much of a choice, but I think I would have learnt all kinds of things if I had done a bit of the socialized childcare with some men around. You see, one of the hardest things is to find your own ways of doing things. I only got to feeling OK about looking after young children when I began to think I was doing it in my own way and not just imitating what women do.

Other Parents (child's point of view)

Some of my fondest memories are of staying round at other people's houses. I was sure for years that a lot of my friends' parents were nicer than mine. I would lie awake comparing all the different kinds of things my friends were allowed to do, what kinds of holidays they had, what they were allowed to eat, what happened when they went to bed. In the long term it was a very empowering thing of my parents to have let me do. They were setting themselves up for comparison. Of course now, as a parent, to think of my own children going to stay with other people feels just a teeny bit threatening! What if my children think that someone else's dad is nicer than me?

Going to stay with friends was something that happened to me after the age covered by this book, but there are plenty of ways you can widen your children's awareness that there are other styles of living. I've found that, right from a very young age, children seem to want to adopt another family or another person. At present my two youngest seem to have adopted Caroline, the illustrator of this book, and want to get over and see her whenever they can. Other times my children have homed in on other parents. Perhaps it's a way of getting looked after without the emotional hassle of your mum or dad breathing down your neck. Where the home your child is attracted to follows the traditional pattern you can, as an active father, come up against some funny situations: you're doing baby talk with the woman of the house and your old friend is sitting there feeling cheesed off and guilty.

See OTHER PARENTS (parents' point of view)

Other Parents (parents' point of view)

I often think of the early days with our first child, going to see some friends who had a child of more or less the same age. It defused all the little petty worries and anxieties and set up a whole new range of the gags and stories that help you cope – like calling newborn babies' poo 'mustard gas', and giving your child's moods nicknames: 'oh, no, he's doing the Screaming Iron Girder Act', a reference to when children go rigid and scream. Their baby was a bit premature, and I also remember going up to the hospital to see him. Barry went behind a glass screen, dressed up in surgeon-type gear, while we looked on. We found that if we shouted, Barry could just hear us. He made a face to show that the baby seemed to look a bit down, so I shouted through the screen: 'Tell him a joke.' Barry mouthed 'What?' 'TELL HIM A JOKE.' Barry looked puzzled. 'ASK HIM, WHERE DO FROGS CHANGE THEIR SKINS?' Barry leant over the incubator and I saw him say, 'Where do frogs change their skins?' He looked back at me. 'IN THE CROAKROOM,' I shouted. Barry went back to the incubator. 'In the croakroom,' he said to the baby.

The baby flourished: now he's fifteen and over six feet tall. It was that first joke that did it.

Pets

Young children love pets. Pets don't always love children. Great big dogs seem to think they're very important, and protect them from strangers. One Great Dane I knew (!) would never let a stranger stand between the mother and the baby in its pram. It wasn't aggressive, it just nudged in and made sure you couldn't get near. Just as well it wasn't aggressive – it was about as big as a donkey.

Cats don't seem to be useful. Young children like poking cats, and cats seem to think that a poke is worth at least a spit and at worst a scratch. Small children and cats clearly weren't designed to be good friends.

Gerbils are a winner if you feel you can look after them as well as a baby, but all young children are animal liberationists in so far as they are very keen on opening cage doors.

Beware of dog do. It is lethal, terrible stuff. Young teething children will quite happily chew a shoe or suck their fingers after they've fallen over in the park. Dog do can carry eggs of a parasite that can make children blind. It's a terrifying thought. You have to be vigilant about it.

Look out for jealous pets. They get all down-at-the-mouth and whiny. If you're holding the baby, a dog will sometimes come up and put its nose on your lap to say, 'me, too'. Pets *must* be kept out of the room where the baby is sleeping. Cats will sleep on babies and possibly suffocate them, dogs might bite, and gerbils . . . well, who knows? Jealous gerbils . . . what an idea.

Play

I must have spent hours, days, even weeks down on the floor building towers, playing dollies' dinners, car races, lego houses or whatever. Play is vital. It's the starting point of all learning. Sadly, its status is low in our culture, where talk is of pushing children from level to level and measuring them in terms of skills acquired.

A lot of adults treat children as if they are really incomplete human beings, waiting to grow up. Evidence for this, they seem to think, is that they don't do real grown-up things, like driving cars, but spend a lot of their time playing. Playing, then, is seen as something childish, unimportant and silly. If you recognize any of this as something you've thought, then now is the time to banish it.

My position is this: we learn through play. Play is where we try out different ways of doing things, in as enjoyable a way as possible. Through play we find out what we can do. Good play breeds more play, more confidence, more ability. Children are brilliant at this and we should help them play in as many areas as possible: with toys, with paper, pens, pencils, crayons and paints, with words, with movement, with climbing apparatus, with voice, with drama, with machines, cooking, and any safe process around. All art, construction, scientific discovery and invention has its origins in play, and in people who are prepared to play.

If you have only one child and this child does not have plenty of other children to play with, then it's you that's got to do the playing. Get down on the floor with those bricks, with the crayons, with the cars and push them around a bit. Think like a child, don't pressurize, don't organize – just play along-

side, adopting suggestions that the child makes: 'Let's feed dolly with a straw.' 'Yeah, let's.'

If you want to occupy your mind with what's going on here, you can see all kinds of concepts being put into place by the child: relationships in space and time, force, momentum, structure, stress, strain. If you get into dramatic play, once again you will see concepts – to do with power, punishment, anger, care, cruelty, fear, kindness – all being worked through in the games. It can get you wondering about stories, films and plays and why we listen to and watch them, or why we don't, as adults, act out power, punishment, anger and the rest.

If you don't want to get into the theory, then just let yourself be a child and enjoy it and see what comes up. Don't take my word for it that it's 'important': play with playing and find out what it means.

Some fun things to do:

- Use dolls, or socks as glove puppets, to do little plays. Remember, you're not into making complete dramas, just little open-ended dramatic contexts. If you listen to children in dramatic play, it keeps going one step forward, two steps backward: they set up a situation, start to act it out and before it finishes, they revise and start up again.

- Buy an easel, loads of sugar paper, a big polythene sheet, plastic aprons, loads of brushes, paint and pots.

- Get toys that offer up possibilities of role playing around them: post offices, houses, people, schools, doctor's sets and the like.

- Get toys that offer up multiple possibilities of construction and shape: play-dough, clay, plasticine, sand and water, blocks, bricks, lego, meccano, construx, quadro.

- Get children into contact with climbing, swinging, pulling and pushing, bouncing, trampolining, dancing.

- Play word-games, do silly talk, make funny noises with your lips, fingers and tongue, go for rhyming, magic words, pretend-words, back-slang, turning words round, spooner-isms, rude words in wrong places.

- Tell stories about the child, listen to stories they tell, write or type them as they are telling them so that you can read them back.

- Have various banging, blowing, plucking and key-pressing instruments that make all kinds of different sounds. Have band sessions to make music.

- Don't get too pedantic about rule-bound games with little ones. Just have matching and finding games.

With very young children, be absolutely fanatical about safety. Examine each toy for its potential to break or fall apart and for bits to get stuck in throats, gouge eyes out, or disappear up noses, in ears or elsewhere. If friends or grandparents give toys that look dangerous, or for too old a child, then simply put them on the shelf for later. As I am writing this, my seven-year-old girl has just fired a sponge gun (that the fourteen-year-old bought for the ten-year-old) into the face of the three-year-old . . . (see PUNISHMENT)!

As a postscript, men are at a possible advantage here. If we really are the immature twits who like kicking bits of leather round fields and hurling darts at the wall that women some-times claim we are, then now is the time to cultivate this spirit. If it exists, play with it. I play, therefore I am.

Playgroups

At the first playgroup I turned up at, a woman called Sue told a story about how she got so fed up with her bloke arriving home late Saturday night and pissed, she tied a knot in his pyjama trousers. Then when he came back she had the delight of listening to him hobbling about at the end of the bed swearing and cursing, struggling to get his legs into the pyjamas. Rather curiously, at the same time another woman there was talking in great detail about the imprisonment of Rudolf Hess.

Playgroups are, quite rightly, story-swapping time for mothers. Then suddenly, out of the blue, comes an alien: a father. Out of the window go all those chats about stitches, pissed husbands, and exercise videos. You are an inhibiting factor. This means that playgroups can be lonely places. Should I be here? Why am I here? How long will it go on? Why doesn't anyone talk to me? Try them if you're prepared to be any of the following: an outsider, or an expert on cars, men's birthday presents, what makes men want to have it off with women other than their wives, how to get boys to pee standing up, and the effects of beer. The other side-effect I noticed was that I was being held up to other husbands as the street goody-goody.

In spite of all this, the little ones usually have a good time and it gives you a chance to see how other people handle their kids, or find out what little tips they've got on where to buy a raincoat. You also see how your child gets on with other children. So if you can cope with embarrassment, it's worth it. It also tests your nerve. Can you stay cool when another kid is poking yours in the eye? Do you stop your kid hoarding tractors and trikes and fighting off nice little children with his

King Arthur's sword? Do you single out one kid, spot the way he rides his trike over other children's feet and dub him a pathological maniac on the verge of a nervous breakdown, drug abuse and murder? Do you hate his mother because of it? Do you want to yell 'SHUTTUUUUUP!!!' at the kid who keeps coming up to you and banging a drum in your face? Do you get in there, start building a lego fairy house and then get upset when none of the children want to play with you? These are some of the pleasant emotions you experience at a playgroup.

Post-Natal Depression

Because this is something that women are seen to suffer, it is inevitably treated as a woman's complaint. However, it doesn't take much imagination to see that being pregnant involves at least two other people: the father and the baby. It may also involve, historically, the mother's parents, the kind of pre-natal care received from midwives or doctors, the kind of labour, the kind of people who were at the labour.

Clearly, for two people to care for a baby together, they also have to care for each other. In the nine months on either side of a birth, most women find desertion, lack of support, indifference, contempt, bossiness, coldness, and so on, almost unbearable. The problem may sometimes be that we never intended to express such feelings, but that's how they came over, and that's how they were taken. Maybe you didn't turn up at a pre-natal class, maybe you came home later than you said, maybe you sit staring at the wall because you're worried about the birth or the baby or money. Everything's very raw and sensitive and feelings of isolation, helplessness, loneliness or an overwhelming sense of weakness and lack of control can lead to a full depression.

What this is all getting at is that, one way or another, we are part of the problem, and part of the solution. This is not to say anyone's at fault, but that to blame the victim, the mother, is precisely what is wrong with, say for example, telling a depressed mother: '*You* ought to see the doctor about it'. Maybe 'we' would be more helpful.

However, if things were as simple as that, there would be no problem. Just to make it really foggy: perhaps you think that what's being asked of you is too much caring, too much support, too much sensitivity. 'Why,' you might ask, 'do you need to rely on me so much? Perhaps the reason why you're getting depressed is because you expect too much from a man. If you didn't expect so much, you wouldn't feel so let down.'

So we are back to that old conundrum of what people feel they are entitled to ask of each other. It's my experience in situations like this, that one partner (or both) appeals to the outside world, citing other couples or experts as evidence that what they are asking from the other is normal and OK; meanwhile, the opposing partner appeals to the outside world as evidence that what the person is asking for is abnormal and unreasonable. It's at moments like this that you realize the word 'love' may simply mean 'equilibrium': two people agreeing on what they think each is entitled to ask of the other. Then a baby comes along and you're trying to work out equilibrium between *three* people. Hard.

Potty Training

This is not a competition. But stand by for the great potty-training races. Conversations with friends soon get down to, 'Oh, isn't he dry YET?' You are soon left thinking that really it's you that's still walking around in nappies. Tough it out. If we make children feel under pressure about their pees and poos, they'll feel under pressure about a lot of other things as well. Peeing and pooing shouldn't be a burden to children, or a performance done to please others. Ideally, the child should get a sense of satisfaction from a job being well done. If you leave potty training to a time when a child *can* appreciate how well it has done, then that is a tremendous confidence-booster, and a cause for self-congratulation to the child.

This said, you may have very little to do with it. You may find, if your child goes to a minder, that the minder is pretty desperate to get her charges out of nappies and 'get them dry' in about two days flat. This didn't stop one of ours needing a nappy at night till she was six, and she would quite often wet herself during the day till she was four. Another one just decided that he wanted to have a go at doing it in the toilet like his older brother, and nothing would stop him. He genuinely did it all himself. My youngest thought that he would keep nappies on till he was three. I suspected he was using it as an excuse to say 'I'm still a baby', so to start off I reasoned with him: 'Don't you think it would be a good idea if you didn't have a nappy? Mummy doesn't wear a nappy, Daddy doesn't wear a nappy, Postman Pat doesn't wear a nappy, the Teenage Mutant Hero Turtles don't wear nappies . . .' and so on through everyone else he knew. This had absolutely zero effect. He clearly thought, 'Yes, I know that Leonardo and Postman Pat don't wear nappies, but I do.'

So I did something that may seem to contradict the self-confidence bit (but remember, he was three). After leaving potties about for a few weeks, and getting him to watch the rest of us on the loo, one morning when I got him up, I took off his night nappy and he walked about with nothing on. I said, 'Tell me when you want to do a wee or a poo.' I figured that he had never really had to think about the actual business of doing it: what it felt like, and so on. Sure enough, first time he wee'd on the floor or, more accurately, on his feet. I don't think he knew what it was at first. I got there with the potty about half way through, to show him that it is possible to catch it. Next time, he called out just as it was beginning so I got there earlier. The third time, he called out just before. Each time, whoever was there made a big fuss of him and said how well he had done. By the fifth or sixth time, he was going to the potty and doing it in there, and he came and showed us the wee or poo he had produced. Huge applause.

Of course, they are never completely dry. Accidents happen when they are so engrossed in a game they leave it too late, so you have to keep an eye open for boys hanging on to their willies and girls crossing their legs. The first few days at nursery or school sometimes need taking gently, with plenty of showing them the toilets and practising sitting on it. Try very hard not to get ratty about accidents; the more ratty you get, the more likely they are to do it again. Whatever you do, don't go in for leaving them in their wet knickers to punish them. On several occasions I've told mine the story of how I was woken up one morning by a phone call from a publisher telling me that my first-ever book was accepted, and as I was standing taking the call with no clothes on, I found it impossible to hang on any longer . . .

If your child is repeatedly wetting itself during the day, then he or she is trying to say something to you about something they're worrying about, such as being bullied at school. Whatever it is, it's unlikely to be anything to do with weeing itself.

Preparing for Fatherhood

One of the first things I found when fatherhood hit me was that, yes, there were things I ought to do, but I couldn't. These consisted of being able to drive a car, earn money, mend toilet cisterns and carry heavy weights. On the other hand, I was good at winding, changing nappies, and putting the baby to sleep. I understand full well that the reverse is probably the case for you. You *can* drive, earn money, mend toilets and carry coal-sacks – all very useful fatherhood qualities, as I've since found out.

So, assuming you've got those before you start and won't be picking them up as you go along like I have, then how do you get your mind round the stuff I *could* do? May I suggest you take up spying? I'm assuming, here, that your partner is pregnant and you're beginning to wonder what the hell is going to hit you. Is the whole thing a dreadful mistake or is it going to be fantastically excitingly brilliantly wonderful? Or something halfway between, like boring? Are you going to be able to carry on marathon running, mountain climbing, ballroom dancing, crossword solving, hang-gliding and part-time brain surgery?

Back to the spying. Very furtively, start father-spotting. When you're out, see if you ever see any men pushing a buggy. Study their faces. Do they look like they've been conscripted by a woman who knows what she wants, or do they look like volunteers? When you go to a party with old friends who have had a child, listen closely to the way they talk. Have they gone completely crazy over what looks to you like a slow-moving piece of pastry? As the baby screams, needs changing, feeding, cuddling or whatever, watch closely who moves first, mum or dad. Does he know where the clean babygrows are?

All questions concerning men and childcare can be reduced to this vital one. In the moments of self-doubt in the middle of the night, in the midst of being asked when it's due, let your mind ask yourself that key question, 'will I know where the babygrows* are?' After you've cleared up that problem, everything's a pushover.

* My editor says: 'Will they know what a babygrow is?' They are stretchy boiler-suits for tiny humans, coming in various colours and patterns including a very fetching convict suit.

Punishment

The old slogan 'You wait till your father comes home' is alive and well. I heard a little boy on the train silenced with it, the day before I wrote this. It's a short-cut to disaster. It signifies dad is the real tough guy in town, while mum is a tender wimp. Mind you, thinking about it, *I* have actually used 'you wait till your mother comes home' to great effect!

Still – no one is perfect, and we are all at our least perfect when it comes to punishment. Everyone gets some of it wrong some of the time, and some of us get it wrong a lot of the time, but most of us think we are doing a better job than most other people.

Wrong things I've done: hit children, mocked them, made them feel small, made other children laugh at the one 'in the wrong', shouted too loud, persisted in being angry long after it was right to do so . . . and I'm sure many other things, too.

Wrong things I think other people do: bribe and blackmail children to be good, lose the power of their punishments by going for the highest stakes too soon, pass on the heavy-duty punishment to another person – nearly always the man.

The great debate between adults, in my experience, is in and around what is permitted. My first memory of my fourteen-year-old's best friend is of him at about eighteen months old, standing in the middle of the dinner table sploshing gravy and carrots all over the place. At the time I thought that this was right out of order, way over the top, permissiveness gone mad. I guess the boy's mother thought he was learning through PLAY about serving people.

One of the first bits of shouting and punishing I went in for arose out of panic. My first child was about eighteen months old and I was in the garden of my parents' home. One moment he was in the garden too, and the next he had disappeared. I rushed round to the front of the house and he'd opened the garden gate and was running up the middle of the road, laughing and giggling with excitement. I reached him just before he got to a junction with a fast-running main road. Yes, I shouted and raved, which may or may not have discouraged him from doing it again. Yet, quite clearly, it was my fault he was out there in the first place.

A similar thing happened just recently. I was proud of myself for having picked up a computer very cheaply, and I put it in the room where the children mostly play, saying: 'It's all yours.' Within 24 hours it was smashed. The three-year-old had stuffed a balloon and a toy car tyre down the disk drive. My wife steered me away to a far corner of the house to meditate on computers, three-year-olds, and stupid parents who leave expensive gear too near to them. The most he experienced by way of punishment was a long, boring trip to a computer repairer's. The guy there sorted him out with a bit of eye-balling.

Some fathers reading this may wish to avoid some of the punitive rubbish they experienced when they were young. Surely there must be a better way of going on, and not making children's lives miseries? All this is very much to do with What is punishment for? Why are we punishing children?

Here are some possible reasons:

- to try to make the child behave more like me
- to stop the child hurting itself or other people
- to make the child feel small
- to defend adult space into which children shouldn't trespass
- to make the parent not look bad in public
- to satisfy the norms of institutions outside the home: school, church, granny's house, shopkeepers, etc.
- to make the child learn and concentrate
- to stop the child lying
- to stop the child stealing
- to stop the child from being lazy
- to get the child to eat some particular kind of food

The question now arises as to whether punishments will actually achieve any of these objectives. What punishments do you have?

- shouting no
- hitting in all the various places, with all the various forces
- giving lectures
- withdrawing affection
- ordering TIME OUT
- withdrawing favours
- demanding forfeits in terms of money, work, apologies, explanations
- bans
- restrictions
- swearing

Some people think that rather than treat every crime as if it must be confronted then and there, you should use diversion tactics: your child hits another – don't hit your child as a punishment, since all that does is confirm that you think hitting is a good and potent way of solving problems. What is better, say the diversionists, is to direct your child to something more constructive, like having a cuddle, building a bridge, or jumping up and down on the trampoline.

What it comes down to is that you don't want your child to be horrible and you're trying to figure out ways to bring this about. The problem lies a lot of the time in the fact that children *want* to be horrible. This is in order to express their anxieties, hates and guilts, and in order to find out whether you're capable of really looking after them. If, for a moment, you can stand back and look at a child being horrible, it's worth trying to think *why*.

Here are some of the reasons why my children have been horrible. They've been:

- angry that an older sister can make something that looks better than what he's done
- angry with a younger sister for getting affection that she thinks she didn't get
- repeatedly doing what she's been asked not to do in order to see if mother is strong enough to keep saying no

- angry that you've been away
- lying out of fear that the punishment will be too severe
- being madly rude when visitors come so as to challenge parents in public
- telling tales in order to jockey for favours
- not wanting to stick to agreed limits in order to test parental strength

The 'crimes' I think worth dealing with are ones where the child is trying to hurt someone (including me) physically or emotionally; where the child is trying to deceive people in a malicious way; stealing; not abiding by agreements.

The sanctions I favour, but by no means have the strength or wisdom always to stick to, are:

- TIME OUT
- Withdrawal of favours

Here's a bit of standard two-year-old's carry-on. He's sitting on my lap and suddenly he attacks my face: a quick poke in the eye, heave on the ear, blowing a raspberry up my nose. No point in yelling, no point in hitting back – best thing is withdraw the favour: 'No, you're not staying on my lap, you've just hit me in the face.'

Another one that crops up is a bit of mucking around just as you're about to leave for somewhere. Say you've agreed to go out together and she starts flinging things around. Sit down and, 'No, we're not going to the park, you've just thrown orange juice all over the floor.' One of ours used to go in for a great wailing and moaning and running away just as we were about to leave for a friend's house or the zoo or somewhere. I think it only needed one cancelled outing to avoid becoming prisoner to such tyranny.

- Demanding a spoken admission of what has actually been done – 'I shot the sponge gun in his face' – because young children especially find it very hard actually to admit exactly what they have done wrong, and a quick 'sorry' is sometimes a get-out.
- Making warnings and ultimatums and being consistent and firm about them: 'If you do that once more, then I'm not reading you a story.' *If he does it once more, then you must, must, must stick to your threat. If you can't stick to a threat, don't make it.*
- Not giving in to children's blackmail: roaring, yelling, spitting, tearing, and punching when the child can't get its own way (see TERRIBLE TWOS). Not giving in is of course a kind of punishment, and it's important to insist on agreed ways of asking for and getting things.

Sanctions I resort to but don't think are in the long run effective or right, and probably create as much long-term horribleness as they avoid:

- Shouting your head off: this at least sometimes has the advantage of making you feel better, and there is something to be said for not having to pretend you're not angry.
- Hitting: sometimes I've rationalized this by making the hit not hurt, as in the tap with a finger on the back of the hand to indicate disapproval rather than causing pain.

- Teasing and mocking: this I've done too often, and for different reasons; sometimes so that I don't have the unpleasantness of getting and feeling angry, sometimes to wage parental power games ('I'm more powerful than you because I can make you feel rotten but you can't make me feel rotten'), sometimes in order to get one of them to admit the crassness of, for example, lying – saying that the cat wrecked my ring-backed diary/address book.
- Making unreal demands: asking five-year-olds to tidy a room, and when they don't, bundling all their toys into a bag and saying I was going to throw them all away.
- Reproducing my own parents' way of going on even if I know I hated it and it didn't work! Hearing your own parent's voice as you wade into action against your own children must be one of the most common and the most unnerving experiences of being a parent. It makes you wonder how many generations back a particular tone of voice, gesture, or expression goes. It could be hundreds of years, couldn't it?

One of the most pleasant experiences you can have as a parent is to go places with your children and have people say to you that they're nice, or that they want their children to come and play with yours. When they're older and they go places without you, friends' houses, school or wherever, and people say that they liked your children, that too is a very nice feeling. There are no rewards, no medals in this business, but when people say things like that, it feels good – even if it enrages you, because the child concerned behaves like a little sod at home!

Putting Baby to Sleep

You may not know this, but you are going to become an expert at putting a baby to sleep. There are several reasons for this:

1. Your wife is so shattered she can hardly move, and though she is the mother of the child, necessity is the mother of invention.

2. You are easily able to adopt a scientific approach to the matter: for example, how many jiggings of a pram does it take before the baby nods off? If the jiggings are more frequent, does that make it easier? If the jiggings are gentler, does *that* make it easier? If you rock the baby in your arms, does it help if you sing? If you sing without rocking, does that make things worse?

3. You don't smell of fresh milk.

Hang on. Don't babies just fall asleep? I hear you ask. Some do, yours doesn't. For some mysterious and infuriating reason, babies don't go to sleep when you tell them to. This calls for much of the above rocking, jigging, singing and the like. Maybe, as you reeled out of a late night movie sometime in the past, you may recall having seen a fairly ordinary-looking bloke rushing past you wheeling a pram. He wasn't a madman, he was a father. He had discovered not long before that wheeling the baby round during the day sent it to sleep. He has therefore made a scientific leap into the unknown by imagining that if he does the same thing at night, the little thing will nod off just the same.

Sod's Law says here that when the baby nods off during the day, it's always just before you need to get it out of the pram. At night, when lucky people are asleep or enjoying each other's love, your little one is wide awake looking at the stars and screaming. A mile or so in the pram will usually do the trick, and if you do it fast enough you will up your aerobic breathing to a fitness-improving level.

Lullabies are helpful; I've heard them described as work-songs, and after an hour of rocking a baby, you'll know why.

A further Sod's Law on this subject is that the first three times you try to leave the child after your bout of rocking, jigging and singing, the baby will wake up again and yell. This is why you will perfect the crazy Nifty Norman technique of creeping away from where you have just laid the baby down. You look like Groucho Marx, without the rolling eyeballs.

Reading Books

Someone with my background is obviously going to say something about this being the most important thing in the universe. The argument is this: the written word remains the main source of formal and theoretical knowledge in our culture in spite of film, TV and video. You want your child to have a chance to get hold of this kind of knowledge because it means access to better jobs, explanations of the physical, biological and human worlds around us, information concerning any operation you might want to carry out at home or at work. The problem is that children, in their normal daily life, don't actually *need* to read: they can play, ask questions, watch TV, and guess.

In the nice little cocoon of the children's book world, it's very easy to imagine that everyone *knows* that children's books are some of the most inventive, artistic and creative around. Bold claim! Just take a look at the art work and design of picture books. Give yourself a chance to see the wit and humour. I promise you, reading children's books can, if nothing else, be a relief from adult work.

One of the reasons I say all this is that there is a very easy trap to fall into, as a parent – just simply buying the books you had as a child. Believe me, children's books have got better and better.

So, if you think reading matters, can I suggest you need to do most of these things:

- Be seen reading and using and enjoying the printed word yourself.

- Right from the time your child is three months old, be sure to have books or book-like things for children to possess for themselves. There are plenty of cloth and plastic bath books around on the market.

- Right from the time the child is very young, six months or younger, find a time, every day, to put her on your lap and open the pages of a book or magazine with pictures in it, talking about the pictures.

- Using a library, the child's school or your wallet, bring at least three books a week into the house. Ideally the child should choose some or most of these.

- Never be a snob and refuse books on the grounds that they're not good enough literature. If you think you know a better or more right-on book, get it as well, not instead.

- Look for books with plenty to talk about in the pictures.

- Remember children need, in very broad terms, two kinds of book: ones that offer images and explanations for the material world around them, and ones that deal in some way with the child's emotional landscape – fears, delights, desires, hopes, and the like.

- Don't be fanatical about keeping books tidy, or the child will be discouraged from browsing and playing with books.

- When you read to your children, don't worry about sticking to every word. It's much more important that it's lively and interesting. Have fun yourself, do mad voices, sound effects and musical backing.

- The cuddle is as important as the reading.

- At Christmases and birthdays, don't lumber them with worthy books; find all sorts of fun things like books linked to TV programmes and films, cartoon books and so on.

- Don't force them to read. Just follow their curiosities about books: they ask questions like, what does that say? Why's that in big letters? Is that a 'B'? Remember that reading is not just deciphering letters, it is about discovering that books are enjoyable and friendly, it's discovering that they tell stories that go from page to page, it's discovering that words and pictures sometimes tell two different parts of the same story.

- It may drive you completely spare but you will probably have to read the same dull book over and over and over again. It's happened to all of us. I think there must be something very important going on here: reassurance? continuity? certainty? some emotional key-point in the text that tallies with something they're thinking about? Anyway, stick with it for as long as you can bear, while looking for alternative thrilling books at the same time.

- When and if you go to a bookshop, of course choose books that you think they'll like, but always give them a chance to choose a book for themselves, too. Put a price limit on it, so you're not bankrupted.

All this may convince you, but of course I haven't offered any guidance here on 'what books?' Some authors and illustrators

to look for with the youngest children: Pat Hutchins, Anthony Browne, Tony Bradman, Shirley Hughes, Errol Lloyd, Raymond Briggs, Quentin Blake, Bob Graham, Beatrix Potter, Rod Campbell, Sally Grindley, Martin Waddell.

Various agencies try to help parents choose books: The Book Trust in London produces an annual booklet called *Children's Books of the Year*, there is an organization run by parents, librarians and teachers called The Federation of Children's Book Groups, an outfit called The Good Book Guide has a children's supplement to its publications, there's a BBC Radio 4 programme, for adults, but devoted to children's books, called 'Treasure Islands', there is a magazine called *Books for Keeps* that is totally concerned with children's literature, and there are several books about reading with children. Look out for the ones by Margaret Meek, Dorothy Butler and Jim Trelease. A historical reference book for the real enthusiast is the *Oxford Guide to Children's Literature* by Humphrey Carpenter.

There are several book clubs that help you choose, and take the edge off hardback book prices. The one that advertises the most is the least satisfactory – it's run by Book Club Associates (BCA) and tends to go for safe and classic stuff. Much better is The Red House Book Club in Witney, Oxfordshire, and for books that reflect a non-sexist, multi-cultural outlook there is the really good Letterbox Library. Addresses for all these organizations and contacts are available from any children's librarian. There! If all that doesn't convince you, then nothing will.

Separation and Divorce

As this is a book about parenting and not about how men and women are supposed to get on together, most of what I have to say about this is under STEPCHILDREN. This leaves out the matter of babies and separation which occurs plenty, too.

First days and months after separation: try to keep up as much contact with your child as possible. If you've got your own place, take your child there, no matter how crummy the conditions. It's the contact with *you* that's important. If you're sharing with friends or a new partner, try to come to an agreement that means you see your child at least once a week.

My situation was that I was living with a new partner, and my children came to stay for half a week. They were 4 and 8. I would spend hours every night reading to them and playing games. Even if it didn't reassure them, it certainly reassured me!

What can happen is that one partner, usually the man, asks for access; the couple weren't married, the woman says no. The point here is that unmarried men have no rights. If it were just a matter of 'yes, if he's seriously interested in childcare, no if he's not', life would be simple. A woman who has a baby on her own may well think she doesn't want to share the child with the disappearing or casual lover, and would rather share it with no one, or with a newly-arriving Mr Reliable.

This said, in the cases I know, the bloke's obvious dogged insistence that he did want to do childcare, that he actually did it and the child was happy about it, won the day. Where blokes have blown hot and cold on the child, not turned up for birthdays, or cancelled things at the last minute, they've not succeeded. No matter how reluctant your ex is to hand over her little darlings to the bloke who ratted, cheated, fell apart or whatever, the obvious luxury for her of having no childcare for up to half a week can prove to be an irresistible temptation. Be unreliable about it, and you'll drive her spare and lose the game.

Nastiness is very popular. One or other of you has got lots of really juicy, horrible things to say. Grown-up children of separated parents nearly all say that this is the most unpleasant aspect of the whole thing. Children want to love both mum *and* dad, and don't want to be recruited for let's-slag-off-ex games.

Perhaps some people reading this will be newly-divorced fathers worrying over whether they can cope with young children on their own, or with a new, childless partner. I've found it really useful to keep reminding myself that parenting isn't something we are born knowing how to do. Women have to learn how to do it, too, though of course many women are conditioned into it early (while we were playing guitars, football, cards and so forth). Most of the other entries in this book are my attempts to say: you can do it. You can bath a baby, handle a raving two-year-old, go round a supermarket with a child, and the rest. In your role as a single parent for half the week, at weekends, or whatever, never be afraid or too proud to pick other people's brains, never be ashamed. If you're looking after a child, there are plenty of people around who will be impressed, even amazed, that you're doing it.

This means that you are entitled to enlist help and support from friends – even ones who haven't got children. A friend of mine who has his child at various times during the week just invites himself over with his little girl. There's no reason why he should sit in his flat all alone with her all day Saturday, when he could come over and see me. He knows that like a lot of other men I forget to make a point of remembering his situation, so he has to do it himself.

Sex

Just to remind you, if you're reading this several months after having a baby: this is what you once did to make the thing that is now stopping you from doing it. I'll take this stage by stage.

Pregnancy – my first thoughts were, no contraception, yippee. Sometimes the foetus joined in and jived about a bit, so it was like doing it with someone else in the room. You may find that your partner becomes more interested in sex than ever before, or you may find she is completely turned off it and what she really wants is lots of stroking and massage. Late on in the pregnancy it's still possible, with interesting experiments in angle. Giggling over this can cause the droop! If your partner is past her due date and getting fed up about it, there's some evidence that doing it brings on labour.

After the birth, stand by to be at your most adaptable and most understanding. Firstly, your partner's fanny may well be heavily bruised, cut, torn, stitched and generally mucked about with. You wouldn't be too keen on eating meat and two veg after having all your teeth out. However, do not fear, the self-curing ability of the fanny is a wonderful thing, greatly helped by rest, good food and kindness. Your partner may not only *not* want to have your willy inside her, she may well not want to play games with it either. Her breasts may be leaky and full, she may be desperately tired and emotionally preoccupied with the new creature, and monkeying about in bed may be right off the agenda. This will be tough on your hormones. Try hard not to get whingey about it, or you'll seem very unlovable.

If and when you get down to it again, stand by for interruptions. Sod's Law here says that the moment you're on the job, the baby will cry. Sod's Law also says that, in this situation, the more caring a father you are, the more likely your willy will shrivel. Your first thought will be 'Is it my turn to get up tonight?', which is not the greatest aphrodisiac in the world – and of course, neither is it for the woman in your life.

There is much speculation on the part of men and women at this time about the nature of the fanny itself. If it stretched to let out seven or eight pounds of baby, how can it possibly resume its glove-like form? OK – the fanny is not a tube, it is a set of muscles. Prior to reading this book, either your partner or both of you may have discovered the mysterious and wonderful pelvic floor muscles. To avoid both leaking wee and the rare complaint of a prolapsed womb, your partner would do well to discover pelvic floor muscle exercises. Both the doing of these and the rather nice consequences may provide both of you with hours of endless fun ... well, not hours, but certainly moments.

As you get stuck-in to toddler-hood and second and third children??? – then other factors come into play. Children and childcare take up an enormous emotional space. If either of you separately or both of you together let it take up all the space, then your sex life will sure as hell go down the pan. As is well documented, this means there's a very good chance one of you will go somewhere else for this pleasure. This means that you have to find time for each other. Always and only meeting each other when children are around seems to be quite a dampener on the libido of at least one partner (see TIME FOR YOURSELVES).

The only thing to say about sex when your children get older is that it's worth remembering that they wonder if you're still doing it, and if so, when do you do it. You may regard this as the ultimate taboo and nothing to do with them, but of course this is by no means a 'natural' response. It doesn't take much imagination to realize that more people than not in the history of the world have experienced jigging away on rush mats, hammocks, bunks, and dormitory beds with other people around, often children.

Sex Ed

The more embarrassed you are about talking about sex, the more likely it is that your kids will pick some awful moment to say things like 'Dad, what's oral sex?'

Decide what words you are going to use. Are you going for the Latin ones or the ones they use? My objections to using the Latin ones are that children don't use them themselves, and you probably don't either – the result being that as you start off on the old penis and vagina routine it all sounds kind of holy. So I'm all for willies and fannies, myself.

No question should ever be avoided. Children from two onwards hear about nearly everything from the news, from older friends and relations and eavesdropping adult talk. 'What's sodomy, Dad?' 'Men putting their willies into people's bums', I said. Then you can get onto what the world and you think about it.

I've found that for all ages of child, books are great. There are books suitable for one-year-olds and up. Children can take them away and pore over them and come back and ask questions. Don't worry desperately if you disapprove of something in a book; you can always buy the book and explain why you disagree with it. Buy several.

I gather that some men think that all this is a woman's job. Strange! There's blokes, traditionally the tellers of dirty jokes, leaving women to tell it how it really is. This has to be wrong. If you have a memory of a dad fudging it and saying, 'Ask your mother' or 'Don't they tell you about this sort of thing at school?' Now's your chance to do better.

Shaming You Up in Public

(See SHOPPING and SEX ED)

If you are the kind of person who can be shamed up (as my children put it), then you can be sure that at some point one of your children will do it. If you've got anything that you don't want known outside the walls of your house, if there's any last remnant of dignity that you cling to, if there's some aspect of your children's psychology that you would rather not everyone in the world knew about – forget it. It'll all come out, and always at the worst possible moment.

My first child rather mysteriously spent the first three years of his life never swearing. There he was in the company of a foul-mouthed, blaspheming curser like me, and the little chap blissfully ignored the lot. UNTIL . . . Nanna came to stay. There we were, round the tea-table, no one talking, no sound apart from the dull clink of cups and the soft splat of jam on scone, and the little chap looks up at solid, respectable, Northern Irish Protestant Nanna and says, loud and clear: 'Fuck'. True to form the good lady ignored it completely, didn't bat an eyelid.

If ever you're trying to do anything furtive, sub-legal, covert, underhand, then you can be sure that one of your children will blow it. I'll admit it: I once nicked a supermarket basket. I hadn't brought enough bags to load into the car, and so I tried to slip away with a loaded supermarket basket. Oh, no. No chance. There he is, the little chap: 'Dad, why are you putting the basket in the car?' 'Shush!' 'But Dad, you're not supposed to take those baskets home.' 'Shuttup!' 'Dad, Dad, you'll get into trouble.' 'Yes, I know I will, if you keep shouting about it.'

'But, Dad . . .' Oh, for a gag.

If you're the kind of dad who's going to pride himself on such things as 'my child doesn't wet herself', then you can be sure she will do just that. Our younger girl wasn't too hot at the old urethra control, and chose great moments to let it all flow. We were in a very nice but slightly chi-chi South American carpet shop in the posh part of Melbourne, Australia. There we were, getting engrossed in llama wool and bilberry dye, and whoosh! She let go of a jerry-can-full. And somehow they always manage to get it in their shoes, so they have to squelch all the way home.

The other one is The Cling. You've been rather proud of the way your child is becoming bold and independent. She's only three, but she toddles off to play in the sandpit all on her own. When you walk through the park, she loves to run on ahead. It's looking good for self-esteem – both yours and hers. In fact, you've been raving on about it, in a rather boring and besotted way, to your friends. Then your friends come over. And for five hours, she never moves more than six centimetres away from your face. She sits on you, climbs on you, hangs from you, heaves on you, jumps on you, and constantly refuses to go off and play with the little son of your friends, even though she spent the whole of the previous month pleading with you to bring him over. You will not boast about independence and boldness again for a long time.

The Cling may go on for years. In its later stages it turns into The Lonely Leg. You're sitting on the sofa, reading the paper, and out of the corner of your eye you notice that your fourteen-year-old son, who thinks eating glass is sissy, has sat down too. A few minutes later you find he's got a bit nearer, and then suddenly his leg flops over and lands in your lap. It's the Lonely Leg.

Shopping

One of the great humbling experiences of my life has been taking a toddler and a baby to do the supermarket shopping, feeling that mixture of pride and clumsiness that seems to go with a lot of this fathering business and watching some super-competent mother whizzing round the place with about four kids in tow. The two-year-old always thought of the supermarket as a place where the acoustics were best for screaming. By the time he got out of the trolley, he'd decided that a supermarket was really a gym. 'Yippppeeeee, look at meeee, Dad!' I called it going Insanes-bury's. I always imagined that people were staring at me, thinking I was brutalizing infants. Old ladies always seem to be the worst. They have a way of showing that they disapprove of everything you're doing, even the way you take the baked beans off the shelf. If you do nothing to stop your kid hurling cornflakes about, they tut. If you tell your kid off for hurling cornflakes about, they tut. If you hurl everything into your bags at breakneck speed at the check-out, they tut. If you take half an hour carefully classifying the shopping, they tut. You can't win.

I've tried shopping *en famille*, doing it with the older kids, doing it all myself, and, the last and most common, ignoring the fact that my partner was doing it all. By far the most pleasurable way of doing it is with the older kids. They manage to get fun out of it, they have competitions, drive you mad about asking for things, but are very good at packing at the supermarket check-out. The least pleasurable is doing the whole thing on your own. It's lonely out there among the cereal packets.

As far as the practicalities are concerned, don't be too proud to take a list. I used to think lists were sissy, but after several rows about forgetting the potatoes, I matured. A male approach to shopping is to copy marathon runners and go for PBs (Personal Bests): best times for door-to-door, best times for getting through the check-out, how many times can you get 100 per cent of the list, and so on. A more female approach is to make it an outing: park the car, go round the other shops, have a cup of tea and a bun, do the shopping, choose something you're going to eat when you get back, eat it, put the shopping away.

One tip: don't admit to your partner that one or more young ladies helped you pack the bags at the check-out counter. It is a firmly held belief among women shoppers that supermarket assistants only help harassed looking guys, and that the same assistants stand and stare at women under similar pressure, as if to say that it's women's work anyway.

Sleepless Nights

Hi there! Have you just staggered into a bookshop, your eyes blurred over with tiredness, looking for some simple easy solution to your nights of hell? Are you just going to read this entry, try to memorize it, put the book back on the shelf, dash home and tell all to your loved one? If so, pleased to meet you. I've done the same, many times. In fact, I think I hold the world record for standing in bookshops reading the sleepless nights pages in baby books. Stick with this page, it might be useful . . . and try turning over a few other pages, if only for the cartoons.

Everyone has his own idea of hell, but nothing comes much worse than this. I remember nights of wandering around crazed, days spent apologizing to people that I couldn't talk properly.

It may be useful to think of it in stages. To start off with, waking up and wanting to be fed is simply what newborn humans do. So, how to make arrangements for this to happen? With my first, we used to take it in turns to get up and fetch him from the cot on the other side of the room, my partner breast-fed him, and we took it in turns to put him back in his cot. The nice thing about this is that it's these tricky moments that help make the child matter to you. As he was our first, it was in the middle of the night that all sorts of crises cropped up, vomiting, coughing and the like, and so it was good to share the panic. I used to have a little homily I muttered to myself (it sounds rather sickening in retrospect) as I was being woken up for the fifth time. Still half-asleep I used to grit my teeth and say under my breath: 'It's the name of the game.'

The tough line on babies and nights goes like this: keep

putting the baby down in its own cot, with its own noises, smells, dollies and little routines and keep leaving it, *even if it cries*. In other words, make it accept a routine that fits your lives and the baby will feel more secure because it knows it has this routine. It's been my experience that people who carry out this method tell you that it works perfectly. Their children, they say, sleep the whole night through, and as you listen to them talking you feel like an idiot and a worm. This may be because you or your partner think it is wrong to leave a baby to cry, but even though you think you're being nicer to the baby, you still can't get her to sleep. But I'm not going to say here that the 'tough line' is right or good because of The Thought (as expressed in COT MOVING) which says: 'the solution you come up with has to suit your way of life and your emotional outlook. If you try to do something you don't agree with but someone has told you works wonders, then it won't work for you.'

So the child gets older and she doesn't sleep through the night. You are getting desperate. You're supposed to be getting up in the morning to go to work, your partner too, and you're both completely shattered, you're rowing about what should be done about it, you've heard about wonderful potions and cures that will do the job, you look in the mirror and cannot believe that a face could turn so quickly into a scrotum. Are you part of the solution?

What follows only really applies to children who have begun walking and talking, i.e. after 12 months or so (unless you're part of the 'tough line' school).

1. If all three of you want to survive, then something has to be worked out that is a compromise for all three. Anything that only satisfies one or two parties will be dynamite for the one(s) left out. I remember lying in bed with a three-year-old kicking my ear all night, then getting up at six in order to tell jokes to children in a school two hundred miles away. In the end, all I could do was tell them about the three-year-old kicking my ear all night, which they thought was by far the best of the jokes.

2. If you haven't gone in for routines so far, then perhaps now

is the time to give them a try. The snag is that because the main reason for the child waking seems to be to get at mum, especially if she has been the supplier of breast-milk and most night comforts so far, then the best person to wean the child off waking is YOU. Hard luck.

3. Here are some don'ts that are worth trying, but they have to be tried every night for at least six weeks to see whether they work.

When you get up for her because she is crying:

- don't give her things to eat or drink;
- don't turn the light on;

- don't pick her up, or at most pick her up for no longer than a few seconds;
- don't get into reasoning arguments about moons, ghosts, or the nature of time.

Instead:

- pat her, stroke her, lie her down;
- sing her the same song, every time;
- say to her something along the lines: it's night-time, go to sleep, here's your teddy, see you in the morning, night night;
- leave the room.

If she goes on crying, decide on how long you will let her cry before going back and repeating the routine. Ideally this shouldn't be too short or too long. Too short is one minute, too long is one hour.

Other tips:

- avoid giving her stimulating food before bedtime, e.g. anything with additives and/or loads of sugar;
- try not to let her get loads of sleep during the day to make up for the sleepless nights: this may mean waking her up after half an hour of a day-time doze;
- make sure she is really having plenty of outdoor exercise;
- try to stick to regular routines about bedtime.

All these routines have to be dropped when the child is ill; a sick child is, of course, entitled to as much night comfort as it wants. However, this sometimes means going back, afterwards, to square one on the timetable.

If you are successful in all this, you will feel like a hero. No other exploits, sexual or of derring-do, will match the buzz you will get for having helped in bringing about sleepful nights.

If, like me, you are not successful, then you can (perhaps) console yourself that the whole thing really doesn't go on forever.

Slings, Buggies, Car Seats etc.

Get down to a big store and check out the technology. In a matter of moments you can spend hundreds of pounds simply catering for moving a baby around for a few months. As you clean out your account, you might wonder how people do it who don't spend that sort of money. A quick glance at an African woman in the street, and you see she has tied a cotton sheet around herself with the baby tucked inside, either on her back or at the side. The western equivalent is the sling. The question you might be asking is, 'Will I feel a prat if I walk down the road with one on?' Well, keep your eyes peeled: more and more fathers are carrying babies in slings and then, especially on holidays, moving up to one of those rucksack baby-carriers. I was proudly carrying my first around in a sling in 1976 and it seemed right at the time, if only because we couldn't afford a pram. The baby feels very protected and snug in there, and you can jig it and pat it in response to grumblings and irritations.

Buggies are now wonderful contraptions rather like Rubik cubes. To use them to their full potential of collapsibility and adaptability you need to be good at wrestling with crocodiles. They are not fantastically durable because they are so miraculously light. You have to have a sense of humour, otherwise you'll kick it when you are trying to fit the rain-hood. My first buggy was nicked by a lady whom I saw in a café about half an hour later. When I said 'That's my buggy', she said 'No, it isn't', and I couldn't think what else to say.

Car seats are much simpler, until you get into someone else's car. For some reason you can never quite work out, you can

only use your car seat in your own car. However, they are ESSENTIAL. You must never travel with a baby on someone's knee, or in a toddler's chair. I know of one child dead and one seriously injured in the last five years because of this.

Carry cots give you the chance to have a bit of adaptability. What you wheel them around in during the day, they can sleep in at night. It's also claimed that a carry cot can be used in the car. BUT you must have security belts for it, and some people say there's a problem with this because the baby can still bounce out of the cot, even though the cot itself is secure.

Prams are a whole world unto themselves. They are masterpieces of coachwork, upholstery and suspension. They are also wildly inconvenient if you've got loads of steps, a narrow front entrance, or a cat (the cat will sleep in it).

So what you have to do is look at where and how you're going to travel with the baby. Ideally, you want to buy all the gear you need, and no more. It's quite frustrating either having something you never use or, alternatively, wanting to get somewhere easily and quickly but finding you can't because you haven't got the right thing.

Don't be too proud to accept gifts or cast-offs, or too snooty to use newsagents' windows for news of second-hand gear.

Smelly Shoulder

How can you tell the difference between an ordinary adult male and a new father? Smelly Shoulder. If you are a keen dad, you will long to pick up your newborn, throw her up in the air, and then listen to the telling-off you get for doing it too soon after a feed while holding her so that she looks backwards over your shoulder. It's then you do little patting things on her back, and you feel all warm and pleased. And it's then that she bloops on your shoulder. It might be a mini-bloop, it might be a mega-bloop, it might even be just a smidgeon of a driblet of a bloop – but believe me, she will bloop.

Bloops are made of milk, and though science tells us that milk takes several hours to go sour, baby-bloop goes sour in about four and a half seconds. For months, possibly years, your shoulder will have little white streaks on it, and you will find that at strange and inappropriate moments a faint whiff of sour milk will reach your nostrils. All kinds of things start smelling of it: roses, car exhaust, lipstick – it's amazing.

Is Smelly Shoulder curable? The terry nappy draped gracefully over the shoulder is handy. A quick change of clothes is OK, but it's better to wash Smelly Shoulder clothes in cool or cold water than in hot, because hot water forces the milk (and smell) in.

Sons and Daughters

One of the toughest women I ever knew once explained to me that all the problems in the world were because of 1. the family, and 2. men in the family. She then went to the States and was last seen in a blind panic because her daughter didn't have a pink babygrow.

I have to say that when I see a three-year-old girl in little patent-leather shoes with heels and a tight skirt, or hear a parent saying to a little boy at playgroup, 'You go and sort out that Jason. Punch him, son', I find myself thinking about what part *I* play in making *my* children stereotypes. How is it that I can be party to a daughter not using all of her body when she runs, or a boy solving all his problems by biffing people? In the end, I can't really escape from the fact that there are ways we as parents prevent girls from being courageous and confident and prepared to take on as many strange and challenging situations as boys do, and there are ways we as parents put pressure on boys to be tough and mean and clever and don't-care-ish.

If you feel like getting into all this, watch the different ways people handle their boy babies and their girl babies. Listen to the tone of voice they use to each sex, listen especially to the differences between what parents say when girls or boys fall over and hurt themselves. As far as girls are concerned, I find myself watching to see if the girls get more favours if they play 'little-me', because encouraging *that* won't do them much good. Do the boys get fewer cuddles than the girls? Is there some cut-off point where boys are expected not to want to sit on a dad's lap any more? In case that worries you, my fourteen-year-old, who frequently doesn't feel in any hurry about getting to twenty, will sometimes plonk himself on me.

It's a real nest of vipers, this one, but broadly speaking I think our girls are entitled to a sense of themselves that tells them they can have a go on computers, speak their opinion in public, climb wall-bars, and punch punch-bags, while among other things boys can do it's also OK for them to cuddle teddies and dads, care about babies, dance, and brush their sister's hair. My three-year-old's favourite pyjamas are the Minnie Mouse cast-offs from his sister.

Stepchildren and Half-Children

I don't know the statistics, but we all know people with stepchildren – me, for instance. There's a lot of it about. Meanwhile, articles and books like this one are always being written about 'families', 'parents' and 'children' as if everyone was living in a mummy, daddy, two children set-up. Hundreds and thousands of people are doing the stepchildren stomp.

To the outsider this can seem like the most fiendish complication in the world. You sometimes overhear a conversation that goes like this: 'Mary has to be at Dave's by twelve o'clock on Tuesdays and we have Barry on every other Friday evening, but only if John is in town, and anyway Karen and Tony are terrific with Steven.' I don't go along with trad thinking in this matter. This kind of thing isn't necessarily either better or worse than the trad set-up. As we all know, some trad families are hell-holes of indifference, neglect or abuse, and some step-families and fosterings are loving nests. What counts in all cases is the 'quality of care'.

That said, stepchildren can be hell. Or to put it more equally, some step-parents are horrible. The step-relationship can be fraught. Here are some of the clash-points:

- 'You don't love me as much as your real children', as one of my stepchildren says. They may be right. But then, why *should* you love them as much? To pretend to is worse than admitting you don't. On the other hand, the stepchild is entitled to fairness in all disputes.

  This may also be a cry from the heart about the 'real' dad: 'real' dad doesn't love me (this can be felt even if he died), so because you're the only dad-figure around, I can blame you for the fact that I think my 'real' dad doesn't love me.

- 'Why doesn't his "real" dad pay for that?' I've thought, if not said. This is the basic meat and potatoes of a lot of step-relationships. Various people in the set of relationships around a stepchild are very good at invisibilizing work. While one adult in the business is swanning it at the theatre, the other one might be washing the child's dirty knickers. While one adult is clocking into work to pay for the kid's shoes, the other one might be sitting with his feet up. If only the solution to this kind of problem was simply for everyone to agree that work wasn't invisible. Instead, there are some-times very strong emotional arguments as to why, even though we're all agreed Jim isn't pulling his weight, it's not worth the aggro to make him do so . . . at least, that's what's often said, but maybe this is a cop-out, and on closer examination it *would* be worth the aggro from your point of view.

- An equivalent cry here is 'Isn't it his turn to have him today?' Plenty of people in the step set-ups have pretty complicated arrangements to try to make it fair and right for everybody. There are emotional needs to be catered for, as well as equality in childcare work. If you're going for real equal time share, some people do it by splitting the week on Wednes-day and Saturday night. And elaborate negotiations take place around times when people want to go away for weekends and at other times. Another system, the one we use, goes like this: for one half of the school term, we have them from Monday night to Friday morning, and the second half of the term we have them from Friday night to Monday morning. This means that things equal out over one school term as regards weekends with or without the children, access to weekday school questions, and so on. Holidays can mostly be split equally in half, or swopped. Our principle is: the less negotiation you do, the better it is for everybody, especially as one side of the business may actually quite like the aggro connected with the negotiating.

- 'We don't speak.' Two parties in the business are not on

speaking terms or are at best abrupt, mean, spiteful and revengeful. In this situation it is very easy for the child(ren) to be pawn(s). I'm sure it's been said hundreds of times, but the point is, such a situation causes a split loyalty in the child. No matter how much aggro the parent might feel towards the disappearing partner, the child is entitled to have plenty of (as much as equal) space with that person. Most withholding and refusing rights of access to children who loved both parents are (outside of abuse cases) adult games and nothing whatsoever to do with the child's needs. Excuses like 'we were never married' won't wash.

• A further dimension is added if you have a new baby. Will the half brothers and sisters go mad with jealousy? Will they compete to be nice to it, or will they compete to see who can be the most horrible to it? With my children, it was a very uniting thing. I half expected that perhaps my youngest would feel usurped and would sit around trying to stop me hugging the new baby, or that my wife's older daughter would be even more miffed than when her younger sister turned up. And believe me, that was bad! But no, everyone seemed really pleased. For a start, they spent weeks trying to figure out what their various biological relationships were. Ever since then, they've spoilt him rotten.

Talking

One of the great delights of having children is listening to them learning to talk. If you think about it for a moment, it is almost as amazing as being born itself. We know how difficult it is to learn a different language from our own: there seems to be so much of it – vocabulary, grammar, sentence order, intonation, pronunciation, different ways of saying the same thing, same ways of saying different things, and so on. Somehow or another these little, fairly helpless creatures of one and two manage to pack away this huge rule-system, so that by the age of five they possess the ability to create most of the common structures of the language.

The fun for parents is listening out for the stages in the child's accomplishment of this. It can be great to keep a note of these as they happen. You find yourself wondering, how come the noises we describe as 'goo goo ga ga' can, in about a year, turn into 'want a drink'? Some nice things to look out for are:

1. The first word. Here you can get into furious debates with people about whether a noise that you know means something – like my first child's 'ma', meaning 'I want some of that' – is a word, or whether the first *recognizable* word is the first, such as 'book' with my first, and 'poo' with my third.

2. Mysterious mispronunciations. Here are some of my children's: 'smeenge' = machine, 'waywees' = raisins, 'diddits' = biscuits, 'prets' = breakfast, 'brummer' = jam. Don't correct these; it only inhibits their experimentation with language.

3. Lovely invented word combinations: my favourite here is my two-year-old's swear word, 'bear-poo', to be shouted at horrid food, horrid brothers and sisters and horrid parents, as in 'YOU BEAR-POO!'

4. Improvised singing and chanting sessions: 'red bus coming, red bus coming, red bus coming.'

5. Incorrect stabs at constructions: 'Don't starfish don't have legs?' This from a three-year-old is a stab at trying to construct a negative way of asking a question, as in: 'Starfish don't have legs, do they?' 'Starfish haven't got legs, have they?' 'Don't starfish have legs?' The nice thing about his 'mistake' is that really what he was doing was putting together two ways of asking questions. He was doing one of the most fascinating things in the whole business: constructing words and phrases 'by analogy'. That's to say, if I can use the word 'don't' as a way of asking a question, why can't I stick it in front of a statement that I'm pretty sure is true, like: 'starfish don't have legs'?
Listen out for 'teached', 'bringed' and the like, which apply the 'ed' rule of making things happen in the past. The old way of looking at that sort of thing was simply to see the child as being ignorant, but really it's the opposite: the child is applying knowledge of a rule.

Along with 'getting him dry' and 'first steps', this is one of those bits of child care that turn into competitions. You may well have to sit through nutty conversations in which people pretend that they're really pleased someone else's child is speaking before their own, or on other occasions they pretend to be sorry that your child isn't talking while theirs is. No doubt you've heard it before, but I'll repeat it: just because your child makes noises that sound like words before other children, doesn't make her a genius. And the opposite: just because your child starts talking long after other children, doesn't mean she's stupid. The first recognizable word may crop up at nine months or at eighteen months. There may be a long time, say from one to three, when you and your partner are the only people who can understand the little fellow. All the consonants seem to be muddled. All this is quite NORMAL. Correcting little ones, making them say things 'properly', making them repeat things just because you say so, are all disastrous. Enjoying their singing, their attempts at doing nursery rhymes and finger rhymes, waiting for them to spit out the beginnings of a story without interrupting, are all much much more important.

Teeth-Cleaning

You don't need to clean a baby's mouth when it has no teeth in it, but as soon as teeth appear, then it's a good idea to clean them. No one ever completely avoids feeding their babies something that will rot their teeth.

Teeth-cleaning comes into the category of chores-that-need-jollying-along. When I'm doing the brushing, before they've learnt how, I go in for various kinds of lunacy: 'Say ah! Say eeee! Say pickled onions! Say ah! Say eee! . . .' and so on. It's also nice to get them to choose their own toothbrushes regularly.

When they're very young it's down to you to do the cleaning, so really go for it: 'upstairs at the back one side', 'upstairs at the back on the other side', 'downstairs at the back one side', 'downstairs at the back the other side', 'upstairs at the front', 'downstairs at the front'. If you say all that, then it gives them a check-list to use when they come to clean their own teeth.

Some kids are prone to mouth ulcers. Weleda make a really good mouthwash you can get from health food shops (leaving me to repeat the pathetic joke, 'Take me to your Weleda').

While getting kids to choose their own toothbrushes is good for awareness, watch out for toothpastes. Rather incredibly, a lot of them actually contain sugar!

Teething

For a reason I haven't figured out yet, we are made without holes in our gums for the teeth to come through. This means that as the teeth grow they have to cut through the gums. Quite clearly, this is hell for the person this is happening to, who can be anything from a few weeks old to up to two years before the whole beastly business is over.

Teething babies and toddlers dribble and sometimes get blotches on their cheeks and neck. They wail and rub their ears and sometimes smell of pear drops. Rubbing their gums with your finger can sometimes relieve them, sometimes make them furious.

It seems that at certain stages of teething rubbing the gums with something hard can be a relief to little ones. The theory behind the rusks you buy from the shop is that they are hard to start off with, and when they get wet they don't break off into little hard bits that could get stuck in the baby's throat, but get soggy instead. But watch out for these rusks: they're mostly jammed full of sugar. So as you relieve teething pains, you rot their teeth. Brilliant. This also applies to the gels and so on you can get from chemists.

Toast is a reasonable substitute for rusks, but you'll notice that the child sometimes takes matters into its own hands and grabs dolls' arms, chair legs, spoons – anything hard to stuff into its mouth. One of my mother's favourite stories was about a friend of hers who was studying medicine when their baby was young. At various times, human arm bones had to be rescued from the child's mouth.

Night times can be difficult when a child is teething. You can sometimes tell if this is the problem because of the way they thrash their head about, as well as from the other signals I've mentioned.

Terrible Twos

It's a generally held view that two-year-olds are horrible. This is partly right. Any parent will tell you that from about two years old till about three and a half, there can very easily be daily tantrums, yellings, rages and wobblies over the most incredibly simple things. I remember breakfasts when the two-year-old said I took the cornflakes off the shelf when he wanted to do it, mornings when I said it was too cold to go out without his coat on, evenings when I put the toothpaste on the toothbrush before he had a chance to put water on it first, tea times when I said no more biscuits, and each time it was worth a tantrum.

First thing: don't panic – it's going on in millions of other people's houses at the same time. In fact, the less you panic the sooner the wobbly will die down today, and wobblies in general will pass away. Wobblies feed off parents panicking.

Secondly, remind yourself that nearly every one of these wobblies is about power. It's as if every wobbly is a set of questions: how grown up am I? Are you strong enough to deal with me? What are the limits to what I can do and can't do?

How grown up am I?
This means that we have to keep telling them: no, you don't decide whether it's warm enough to go out without a coat, I decide because otherwise you get ill. On the other hand: sorry I wet your toothbrush, you *can* wet your own toothbrush, because you *are* big enough to do that on your own, and so what if you do spill water on the floor, it's no big deal.

Are you strong enough to deal with me?
Because if you're not, that means I'm stronger than you. I know

I'm just a very small thing who is afraid of loads of things . . . please be stronger than me so that you can look after me.

This means we have to say things like: it's no use you shouting, it won't get you more biscuits. I have decided. If you go on shouting, then I'm not saying anything else to you until you stop.

What are the limits to what I can and can't do?
Because if you don't tell me, or if you keep changing your mind, I won't know where I fit in in this world.

This means saying what the limits are and sticking to them. People imagine that it's the limit itself that's important, when really it's the fact that you stick to it that is important. In other words, it's much worse to say 'No jumping up and down on the sofa' but only stick to the rule a third of the time than it is to let them jump up and down on the sofa all the time, but have something else that you're consistent about.

Sometimes the Terrible Twos seem to last forever. Yes, you may well find that friends shun you, people stare at you like you're some mad sadist when your little darling throws a wobbly in Sainsbury's because you say 'you're not buying a cake this week'. Yes, I have had rows with my partner about what to do, but actually the children have learnt that one parent does it one way, and the other does it another way. That sort of thing matters much less when you're each doing childcare: 'Buy me a bun. Mum always buys me a bun in this shop.' 'Well, I'm not Mum. I'll buy you a bun when you don't nag for one.' And the two approaches can exist side by side. But remember, the Terrible Twos do pass eventually, and the calmer and more consistent you are, the quicker it will happen.

Time Out

This is not your time out (see TIME TOGETHER and GETTING AWAY). It's one of those funky little American terms for something really important. There's usually a point, when children are relating to each other (and to grown-ups), at which the temperature starts going up, voices start getting screechy and things start falling off tables. This is where you bring in 'Time Out'.

Rather than trying to solve the argument, or getting into elaborate negotiations about who really smashed the lego tower, you simply separate the sparring partners. Where this is two or more children, they just have to go to different rooms, to different activities (see INDOOR-ITIS), or simply in different directions. Where this is you and a child, the same thing applies. Sometimes, rather than have a row it is better simply to excommunicate either yourself or the child. So: at tea time, one of the kids is playing up, pushing at the beans ('Don't want beans'), the other kids are laughing, you're tired and ratty and feeling put-upon for reasons you haven't figured out yet . . . what to do? Rather than scream at the offending kid, which will wind all the others up even more ('Hey, Dad, your nose goes red when you get angry'), what you do is simply send the offending one out.

Devise a regular place if you like, preferably boring and unattractive. Don't over use it, but have it as a reference point for all disputes. If the children are fighting while watching TV, warn them they'll get the separation treatment. If you only have one kid then this is a very powerful sanction, because the basis for the argument between you may be about demanding something from you. A lot of rows are really trials of strength, and to pursue the row is a kind of weakness. The way to show that you mean business (in a situation that matters) is to withdraw from the row, take Time Out.

If all this sounds reasonable, and even more – you are actually able to carry it out – there may be one other problem. Your partner may think it's cruel, may think it's unreasonable, may think it's some horrible male way of going on; or, to be fair, may think it's a good idea, but not for her, thank you very much. So you're into negotiations; but remember, you don't have to agree on this. So long as you are doing your stint of childcare, you're entitled to do things your way.

Time Planning: The Caterpillar Principle

This is a metaphor, a symbol for a day in the life of your family. If you're yet to have a child, then I think you may well find that the most valuable commodity in your life will become Time.

Watch a caterpillar. Notice that sometimes one part of it all squashes up and another part stretches. Notice also that it isn't always the same parts that squash and stretch; any part of the caterpillar can do this. And, finally, notice that though the caterpillar appears to lengthen and shorten, in actual fact it is in essence the same size.

Is this useful? Is this helpful? I find it so, though sometimes I call it the concertina principle. The point is, every day is the same length. Therefore:

- The caterpillar needs to be fed. In practical terms this means that there are a set of fixed jobs that have to be done, no matter what happens. Money has to be obtained, food has to be fetched, children have to be attended to, taken to school and so on, and all these jobs are of equal status. This means, if one person doesn't do it, then the other person has to (one person has to stretch more to do more, because the other person has contracted, to do less). Most blokes don't know this, and if they do, they pretend they don't.

- Whatever takes up more time means less time on something else. This means that the longer you stay out, the less time you will see the children, the less time you will see your partner, the more ratty and resentful people will be with you.

- A lot of activities that don't have a fixed length of time will simply expand to fit the available space. This means that if you agree that you both need to do a big clean up of the place, you may *think* it can all be done on Saturday, but it will certainly take the whole weekend.

- Some things that get squeezed out of the timetable today will still be there tomorrow. According to this principle, washing up doesn't go away. Where this principle breaks down is in TIME TOGETHER. Here it is quite possible to squeeze out Time Together today, and the next day, and the next, and it never comes back.

Time Together

So there you are sitting having one of those nice conversations about the world and life, just like you did when you first got together, and every time you try to say something it gets interrupted by a nappy or a fish finger.

Being a caring father and work-sharing round the house may well be a democratic way of running the factory called Home, but it may also be a complete sexual and emotional switch-off. There have been whole periods when me and my partner have only met over a chore, and I have begun to resemble a potato sack. I've started thinking that what I really need is some time for GETTING AWAY. Maybe I was wrong. In order for the whole thing to work, what we actually needed was Time Together.

This is all very complicated. How do you know how to balance what's best for you, best for the relationship, best for the household? Obviously there are no simple answers, but if you never go out together without the children, it might just possibly be the reason why you've stopped being nice to each other (see SEX).

I've always been jealous of people who have relations who love baby-sitting. That's one obvious solution; the only other one is the BABY-SITTER.

TV Watching

Telly gets rationed in our house. This is because if I say to my children 'You can watch as much telly as you want to', they do. They watch all of it, all the time. What does this mean? Mostly, I think it means that in a competition between watching TV and doing homework, talking to me, going for a walk, reading a book, playing with toys, then usually watching TV wins. The point is, TV is very attractive, very clever stuff that very clever, attractive people spend an enormous amount of time, money and brainpower on. When it finally comes down to it, the whole thing looks and feels a good sight more clever, attractive, and expensive than me, or any of us: small wonder they rush off to watch it all the time.

My gut feeling is that in order to operate in the world, children need plenty of practice choosing, making and doing things for themselves. This may be painting, talking, playing with toys, doing little plays, even arguing or fighting or anything else that involves active engagement and participation. The problem with the telly is that the only role it gives us is spectating, which should ideally be only one of many kinds of things a child gets up to. However, if you can pull the spectating of telly into something you talk about with your children, then it is turned into a more active process. The child's view meets someone else's view, and debate and argument challenge the omnipotence of the screen.

All this may seem crazy, thinking of a one-year-old and children's telly. Do you really want to get into a deep discussion with her about *Rainbow* and *Playdays*? Why not?

As an afterthought, I'd say that it's very easy to become anti-telly with children around; they seem obsessed with it, yak on about it at tea time, act out adverts, and burst into tears if they miss their favourite programme. I've found that saying 'but it's only telly' doesn't go down too well. But then, from their point of view it's a shared talking point with all their friends. The more TV they watch, the wider range of talking points they have. As educational experts go about their business, they quite often lament the passing of the time when shared talking points were such things as *Peter Pan*, *Alice in Wonderland*, and Caesar's *Gallic Wars*. What has happened is that children from the age of one and under have built up a *different* set of talking points, and one that parents and teachers have very little control over. Quite often it seems to be this lack of control that is so irritating: 'why do the little blighters take more notice of that berk doing the birthdays on children's TV than of me?' But of course, that is precisely why they take more notice – *because* he isn't me, Dad, the one who tells them off.

It sounds very goody-goody, but if you sit about talking to children, helping them make things, if you take your kids out and do things with them, then at least telly has to compete with life, and isn't left to win hands down.

Weaning and Getting onto Solids

You are in an ideal position to do this, especially if it means coming off breastfeeding. It's actually quite hard for a woman to persuade a little person who has had all the fun and warmth of a juicy nipple in its mouth to enjoy the feel of a spoon and a bit of mashed carrot. Every time she comes for him with a spoon in her hand, he knows that there's a nipple at the other end of the arm – well, nearly, anyway. So, quite often he roars and shouts and tries to get down mum's blouse. (As we know, this kind of behaviour by little boys can carry on into later life – in slightly different circumstances, though the psychologists tell us the cause may be the same.) So you can now move on from being the expert winder to become an expert weaner.

The food: it should be warm and juicy; avoid all additives, salt and sugar (read the sides of jars and tins); preferably use a suitable bit of the food you're having; use a blender if you've got one, though the back of a fork will work perfectly OK on a bit of potato; don't give them egg till they're a year old; in early days, avoid strong herbs and spices – think bland; only introduce one food at a time.

Feeding: the first time I tried this, I'd sit my oldest in the chair and very carefully dangle the spoon in front of his mouth, hoping he'd make a dive for it. Funny thing, he didn't. Then we went to Ireland to meet his Nanna. She was appalled at such pussy-footing. 'You'll never stop nursing him [breastfeeding] like that,' she said. 'He'll be taking you to school with him.' At that she grabbed him, tucked him into the crook of her right arm, held the bowl with her right hand, and started diving in and out of the bowl with the spoon in her left. 'Keep it flowing,' she said. 'Don't give them time to think about it.' It all looked a bit brutal to me, but it certainly worked. It makes sense, because why should the baby have to lose both the nipple (or bottle) as well as the hug and the eye contact?

Drinking is an interesting game. The conventional route is nipple to bottle to sucky cup to real cup. Do you know what a sucky cup is? This is one of those pieces of apparatus which becomes totally indispensable to your child's life, and yet in an odd moment of contemplation you find yourself wondering, did cave people have sucky cups? Probably not. Anyway, they are plastic cups with lids that funnel into a kind of flattened nipple. In the 'nipple' is a set of tiny holes specially designed to get blocked up with the fibres in orange juice, harbour filth and germs on the inside, and be chewed by your child. This sounds very defeatist and cynical, but such a feeling is mild compared to the fervour with which the little ones scream: 'CUPPY-CUPPY! DINK! DOOCE!' with hands outstretched. You will learn to love the sucky cup, the glazed eyes of the child locked on to it, the mad gulping noise from the throat and the soft hissing of air rushing in. Music!

To return to force feeding – this phase doesn't have to go on long, and soon they're sitting in a high chair lobbing food all round the room, playing games by turning their head away just as the spoon is supposed to go in the mouth, so – doink! straight in the ear; keeping their mouth open after the food has gone in, so – gggeee, down the chin; keeping their mouth shut so you can't get the spoon in, and so on. I've had all this and more, and this was when I dug down into the much needed repertoire of funny faces, funny noises, impressions of aeroplanes, birds, octopuses, and songs beginning with: 'here comes the . . .'

Also good fun is when you get onto 'finger food'. Chop up cheese, apple, fish fingers, toast into little cubes and let them feed themselves. This gives them independence and the joy of feeling their nosh. It might mean that they *also* want to get their fingers in the mash and gunk that you want to feed them. Either way, be prepared for gunk, cheese cubes, toast fingers, flying round the room. Whatever you do, never try to pick up this stuff while they're eating, because they'll only lob more just to watch you picking it up – and anyway, while you're bending over they always aim it down your neck. At some point you should let them have their own spoon while you're trying to feed them with yours. This means that sometimes you end up fencing. On the other hand, while they're busy concentrating on lifting the spoon, you can get three mouthfuls in. I remember a woman saying to me: 'If there's one thing I really love, it's seeing her putting away a plate of food.' I know what she meant. Seeing a little child attacking some food with enthusiasm is a really nice thing to watch.

Winding

Two schools of thought here:

1. Winding is totally unnecessary; if they want to burp, they'll burp, so why go through all that flap and palaver? There's no evidence that all that banging and squeezing makes them burp. Anyway, you try getting really hungry, going out to a nice Italian restaurant and being dragged away from a juicy spaghetti bolognaise every few minutes to have your back walloped. Anyway, no one winds piglets, and they seem to manage.

2. Winding helps them feed because their little bellies get full up with air, which stops the milk getting down. Also, if you burp them it prevents the high velocity burp that means total bloop at the end of their feed. Air in their bellies gives them cramps and pain while they're feeding and puts them off their sucking.

Choose whichever line suits you: the little darling will survive either way. However, if you plump for 1. you will find that winding is one of those folk-truths you may find it impossible to argue about with People-who-Know. They may brand you a dangerous hippie revolutionary.

One advantage with winding, it's something you can do (or pretend to do) so that you're not just left gawping at breast-feeding time. However, don't feel that winding equals thumping the poor little thing. I have big hands (you may not), and I found it quite easy to sit the baby sideways on my right knee, supporting it with my left hand round its chest, my right hand pushing up the spine, gently but firmly straightening the back and lifting the rib cage. I suppose what this does is alternately squeeze and release the bag-like stomach. This means success – whether there was a burp in there from the feed or not, the baby'll burp all the same. You may even become known as an expert winder. Gold medals are hard to get in this game, and you'll need whatever's going. Anyway, whatever you do, avoid all that banging and thumping. It must be horrible for the little things.